D0532095

CHESS IN ACTION

Library of Congress Cataloging-in-Publication Data

Mantell, Paul.
Chess in action : from first attack to checkmate / Paul Mantell and Dean Ippolito ; illustrated by Giacomo Marchesi.
p. cm.
Includes bibliographical references and index.
ISBN 978-1-4027-6046-4 (hc-plc with jacket : alk. paper) 1. Chess--Juvenile literature. I. Ippolito, Dean. II. Title.
GV1446.M36 2010
794.1'2--dc22
2009014479

Lot #:
2 4 6 8 10 9 7 5 3 1
02/10

Published by Sterling Publishing Co., Inc.
387 Park Avenue South, New York, NY 10016

Distributed in Canada by Sterling Publishing
c/o Canadian Manda Group, 165 Dufferin Street
Toronto, Ontario, Canada M6K 3H6
Distributed in the United Kingdom by GMC Distribution Services
Castle Place, 166 High Street, Lewes, East Sussex, England BN7 1XU
Distributed in Australia by Capricorn Link (Australia) Pty. Ltd.
P.O. Box 704, Windsor, NSW 2756, Australia

Printed in China

Sterling ISBN 978-1-4027-6046-4

For information about custom editions, special sales, premium and corporate purchases, please contact Sterling Special Sales Department at 800-805-5489 or specialsales@sterlingpublishing.com.

Book Design by Josh Moore
Illustrated by Giacomo Marchesi

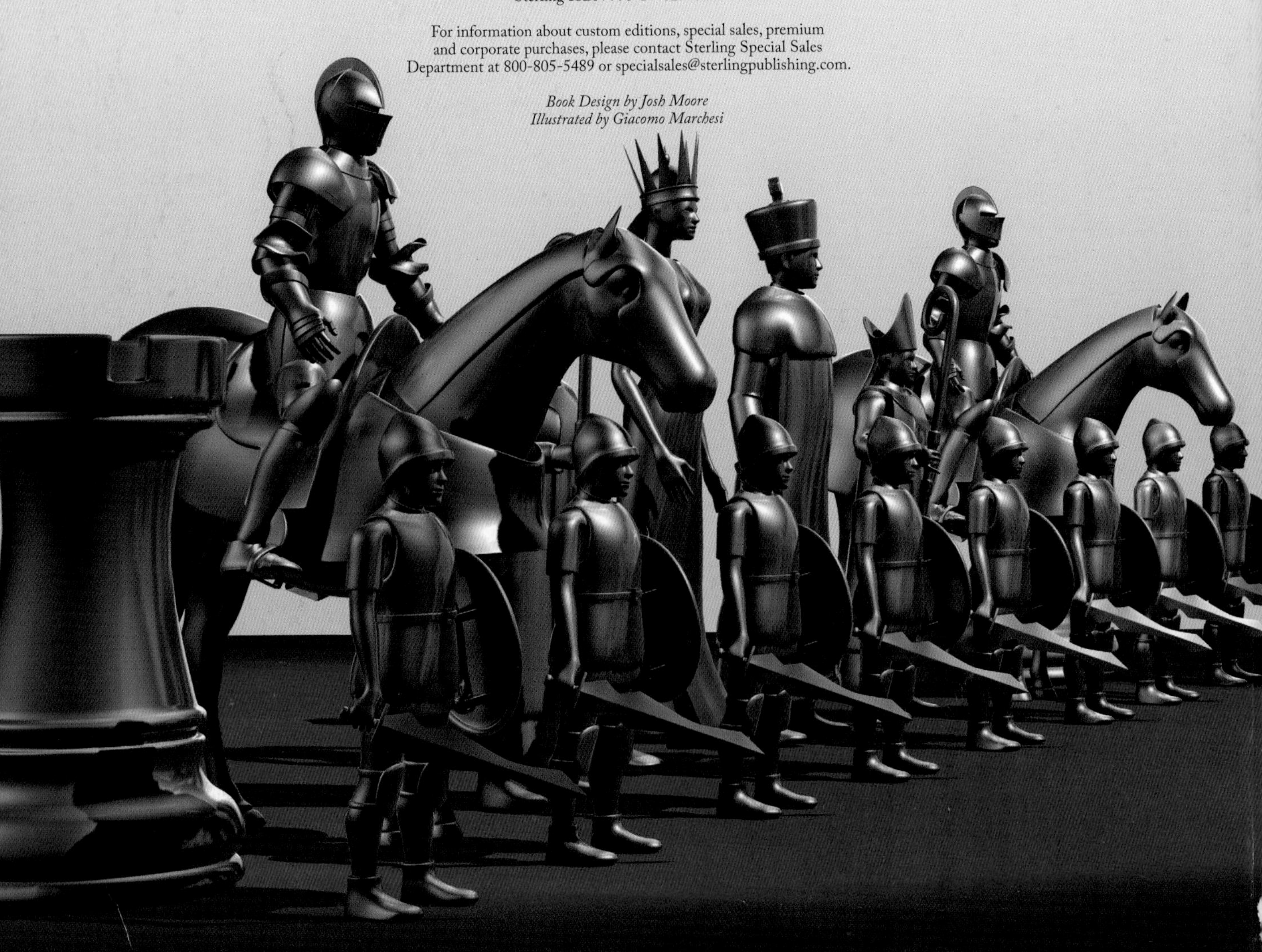

CHESS IN ACTION

FROM FIRST ATTACK TO CHECKMATE

PAUL MANTELL
and
DEAN IPPOLITO, *International Master of Chess*

Illustrated by GIACOMO MARCHESI

STERLING
New York / London
www.sterlingpublishing.com/kids

CONTENTS

NOTE FROM DEAN IPPOLITO

Chess is an exceptional game that combines the endurance of a sport, the precision of a science, and the creativity of an art. I began learning to play chess in 1980 when I was two and a half years old. Both of my parents were schoolteachers who knew the importance of a well-rounded education. My father realized the benefits chess could offer children after he introduced the game to his students. He quickly saw their grades improve, along with their confidence, memory, concentration, and many other qualities that traditional teaching methods tend to ignore. Too young to attend school myself, every weekday I would wait with a chess set in hand for my father to return from work to teach me how to play. I was fascinated with the different chess pieces and their movements on the 64 squares.

My excitement grew when I attended my first chess tournament in New York City's Carnegie Hall at age six. After playing mainly with my father as an opponent, it was exhilarating to see hundreds of other children all in one room, all interested in playing chess. The boards were set up, and I was excited and ready to play. After two full days, the tournament ended, and I celebrated my third-place win over all the first-time tournament players. This gave me a great feeling of success.

Since that tournament, I have played in hundreds all over the world. I've won 12 national championships and have been selected 11 times to represent the United States on the All America Chess Team. I've had to overcome my fear of flying to play international chess overseas, and I've traveled to countless foreign countries where I've made many friends and learned many foreign words, even becoming fairly good at speaking Spanish. I've gotten the chance to meet celebrities in the political, entertainment, and, of course, chess worlds. I was even a member of the Jack Collins Team—Jack Collins was considered the greatest chess teacher of the 1900s.

Chess has also had therapeutic effects for me. When I was six, my father and I were in a bad car accident, and we recovered together while playing chess. I returned to school weeks after the accident, but my father wasn't able to go back to teaching for months. It became his turn to wait for me to come home from school so we could play chess.

Throughout the years, many interests came and went, but chess was a constant. When I was 15, I decided to play professionally after high school. My spirit was tested, though, the year before high school graduation during a time of poor tournament results. I had doubts about my abilities, but I always remembered Thomas Edison's quote: "Many of life's failures are people who did not realize how close they were to success when they gave up." As soon as I decided that I loved chess enough to try to overcome those doubts, my results immediately improved. Upon graduating from high school, I committed myself to improving my game and began playing competitively all over the world.

After playing professionally for five years, I began my own chess instruction organization. With the help of my wife Dawn and ten other qualified, enthusiastic instructors, I now teach chess to several thousand students each year. It's wonderful to see young players appreciate the game for the first time and to help them to develop their skills. I enjoy passing on the valuable life lessons chess has taught me, as well as my love for a great game. I feel fortunate to have been a coach to thirteen national champions and to have been voted the New Jersey Chess Teacher of the Year in 2006 by the New Jersey State Chess Federation.

The benefits of chess for children have been touted by chess enthusiasts for years. Throughout my time teaching, I have seen all different kinds of children enjoying and benefiting from the game. It's a great way to challenge and exercise your mind. Your grades may even improve as your interest and study of chess increases; critical-thinking skills generally improve, as do math and reading-comprehension skills. I have begun to teach chess to my three-year-old daughter, and she already loves the magical pieces, especially the knight.

While chess as a career is certainly not for everyone, anyone can enjoy the game. Chess brings together people from all walks of life. It is one of the only games where you can watch a five-year-old girl playing against a 50-year-old man and have no idea who is the superior player. All chess players can benefit from the mental exercise, the friendly challenges, and the experiences that last a lifetime.

—DEAN IPPOLITO

International Master of Chess

President, Dean Ippolito LLC

A Premier Chess Instruction Company

PREFACE

Chess offers endless excitement, whether you're young or old. There's the challenge of staying one step ahead of your opponent, the pleasure of spoiling his plans with a surprise attack, and the thrill of drawing him into a trap and then striking with a sudden thrust!

People fall in love with the game of chess because they find it exciting. I remember getting hooked at the age of four when my dad sat me down and showed me the basics. Each week we used to play through the games in the newspapers, figuring out how and why the players won and lost. Through study and reading a book or two, but mostly through playing, over time I got better at the game. Soon my dad, who had always let me win in the past, had to think hard to keep from getting beaten by a six-year-old. Imagine my delight at age seven when I beat him for the first time in a game I knew in my heart to be fair and square!

Look at the passion some people put into video games. Now think of chess as an ancient, non-gory substitute that can still hold your attention. The big difference with chess is that the combat is not on a screen, but *inside the players' heads*! In chess, you have to study the battleground

from above and peer into the future to see two, three, or more moves ahead. You have to plan your attack, taking care at the same time to prevent any enemy assaults on your king. From start to finish, you are in command of your army—it's *mano a mano* ("hand to hand" in Spanish), and only one player can come out on top! There's a reason chess is sometimes called "the Game of Kings."

My hope is that this book will offer the game of chess as an exciting alternative to the often-violent images and play we've become hooked on through video games. Chess will still sharpen your brain in countless ways, without any blood (real or virtual!) being spilled.

Whether you become a lifelong chess player or not, the game itself will always live on, as it has for thousands of years. I hope you enjoy learning to play "the Game of Kings."

—Paul Mantell
Co-author and chess enthusiast

THE EVE OF BATTLE

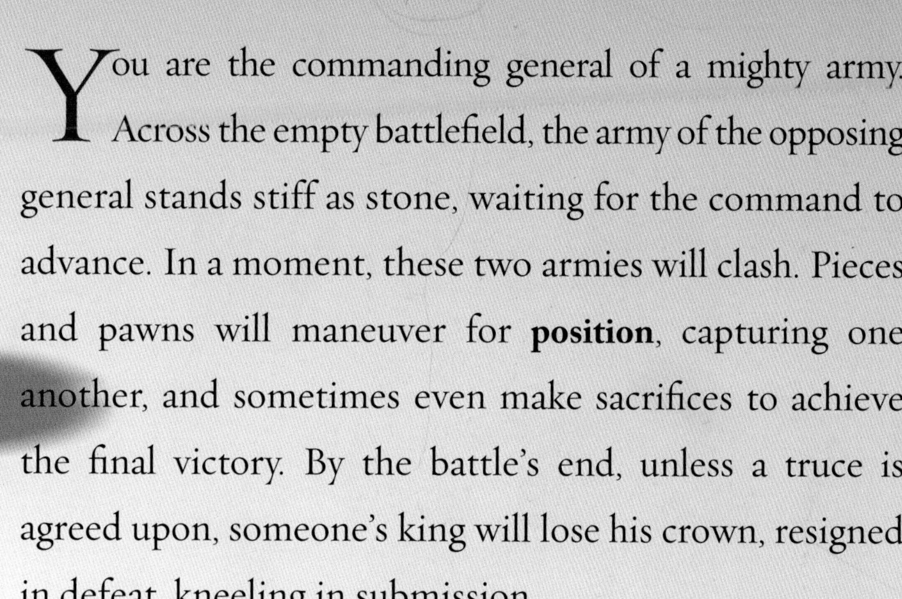

You are the commanding general of a mighty army. Across the empty battlefield, the army of the opposing general stands stiff as stone, waiting for the command to advance. In a moment, these two armies will clash. Pieces and pawns will maneuver for **position**, capturing one another, and sometimes even make sacrifices to achieve the final victory. By the battle's end, unless a truce is agreed upon, someone's king will lose his crown, resigned in defeat, kneeling in submission.

No, it's not World War III. It's not the latest video game, either. You're playing the ancient and noble game of chess—and the battle is about to begin!

Whether you are a complete beginner, or a **grandmaster** dueling for the world championship, the excitement of doing battle across the chessboard is pretty much the same. There is no actual blood spilled, of course, and that's a good thing.

But just because no one gets hurt doesn't mean the combat isn't intense. You don't get extra lives in chess the way you do in video games. When a player's king is "checkmated," the game is over. But you and your opponent, the two commanding generals, live to fight another day.

And you *will* fight again because once you have felt the thrill of chess combat, you'll be a player for life, just like millions of others who have enjoyed "the Royal Game" over the centuries.

Young warrior, though in the end you must win your chess battles alone, this book will start you on your way. May its lessons be in your heart and in your mind when you first go into battle.

From now on, consider yourself a general in training!

A BRIEF HISTORY OF CHESS

As a chess player, you are joining a long line that stretches back through the mists of time. "The Royal Game" seems to have first been played in northern India, about 1,500 years ago. From there, it spread to the nearby Persian Empire, which stretched from modern-day Pakistan all the way to the Mediterranean Sea.

When Islamic warriors conquered Persia, Africa, and Europe in the eighth century, they came to stay, settling in those lands and intermarrying with the locals. They also brought their favorite game with them. Soon the local nobles were playing it, too. Everywhere it spread, and chess became a favorite of kings, lords, ladies, and other members of the upper classes, who were the only ones who had time for playing board games (in those days, most people were busy working hard just to survive).

During the Middle Ages in Europe, some changes were made to the game. The pieces, for instance, were given the familiar names we know them by today. What had once been the powerful *caliph* (Islamic "emperor") became the king. The *vizier* ("prime minister" in the Islamic world) evolved into the mighty queen, able to move many squares at once instead of just one at a time. Other ancient pieces, such as chariots, horses, warriors, and elephants, became bishops, knights, pawns, and rooks (castles), all very well known figures in Europe in those days. The 64 squares of the chessboard became alternately dark and light, as they are today, instead of being all the same color.

It was only in the nineteenth century, after the Industrial Revolution created a middle class that had time for occasional fun, when chess became not just a royal game but a pastime for everyone. We'll go more into the modern history of chess in the section titled "Championships and Politics" (page 94).

THE CHESSBOARD

The "battlefield" of chess is the chessboard, and it may seem familiar to you. If you've ever played checkers, or even seen a checkerboard, then you already know what a chessboard looks like because they are exactly the same!

The board consists of a large square divided into 64 smaller squares, alternating between light and dark colors. To avoid confusion, the alternating shaded squares on the chessboard are referred to as "light" and "dark," *not* "white" and "black." It's the **pieces** themselves that are called "White" and "Black" no matter what colors or shades they actually are.

To make sure you've got the board lined up right, turn it so that both players have a light square in the near right-hand corner. Remember: "Light on the right." Got that? Good.

Now, notice that the 64 squares on the board line up in eight columns of eight squares each, stretching from your side to your opponent's. These columns are called **files**.

Files are identified by the letters "a" through "h," starting on White's left and ending on his right. If you're playing Black, it's the opposite: the "a" file will be on your far right, the "h" file, far left.

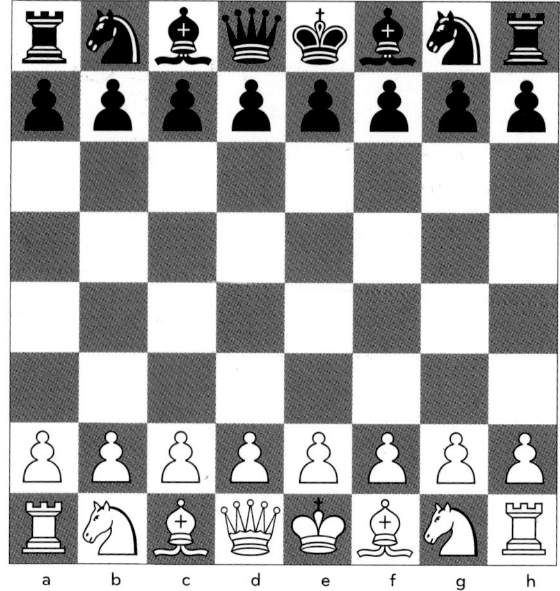

There are also eight rows going across the board. These are called **ranks**, and they are numbered from 1 to 8, starting from the rank closest to White.

Ranks 1 and 8 are referred to as the "**home ranks**," or **back ranks**—1 is White's back rank and 8 is Black's.

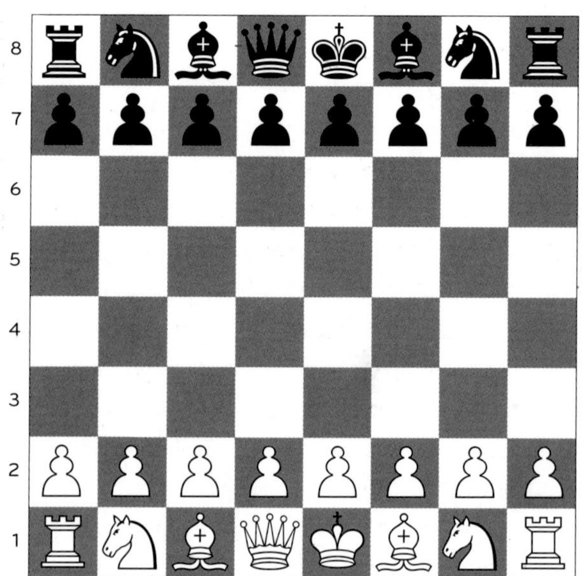

Here is a **diagram** showing how the 64 squares on the board are identified. Each square has a letter and a number attached to it, showing its file and rank. No two squares have the same letter-number combination.

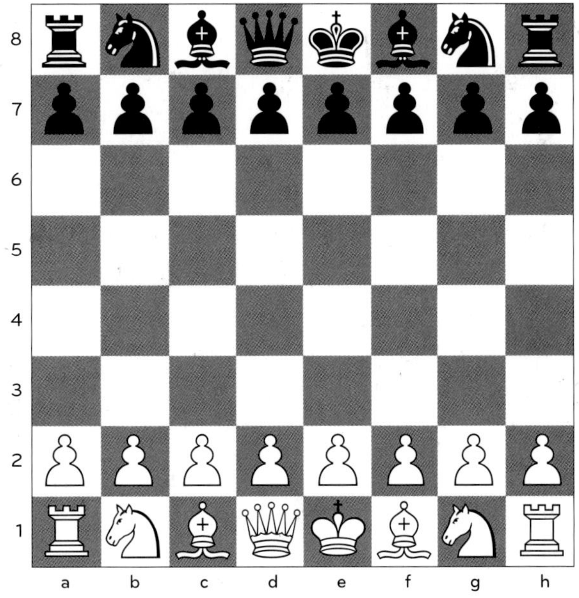

Notice also that there are **diagonals** of same-colored squares that crosshatch the board. Each diagonal is made up of either all light squares or all dark squares. In chess **notation**, which we'll discuss in a moment, these diagonals are identified by the letters and numbers of the squares at either end. For instance, try to locate the diagonal a1 to h8. It goes from White's near left-hand corner to his far right-hand corner. It's a very important diagonal to control because it contains a great many squares. Compare it to, say, diagonal g1 to h2.

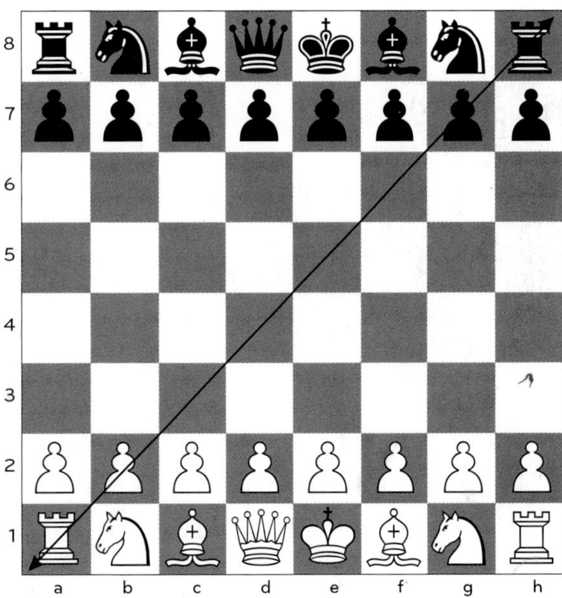

We'll come back to diagonals later, but the main thing is not to forget them because when it comes to playing the game, they can be just as important as ranks and files, especially those really long diagonals.

CHAPTER ONE

SETUP AND SOLDIERS

NOW THEN, GENERAL, BEFORE WE BEGIN STUDYING the game, let's take a closer look at your army and its different kinds of fighters, or **pieces** and **pawns** as they are called. Pawns and pieces are not always developed, or brought into the game, in the following order of introduction, but here are your 16 soldiers:

PAWNS

Standing shoulder to shoulder at the start of the game, your eight pawns are your foot soldiers, and they await your orders. They will sacrifice themselves at your command. Like a sturdy wall, they will put themselves between your king and mortal danger.

But pawns can only do so much. They are limited in their powers and abilities. If you're not careful to position your pawns skillfully, they can block the movement of your own pieces, trapping them and making them useless.

Pawns can only move directly forward, never backward or sideways. Their first move can be either one or

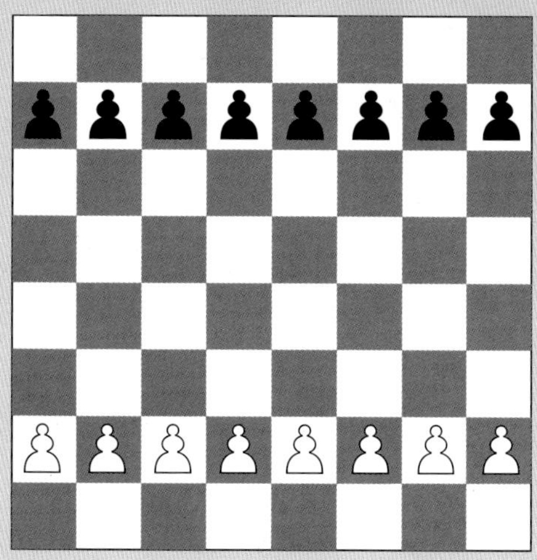

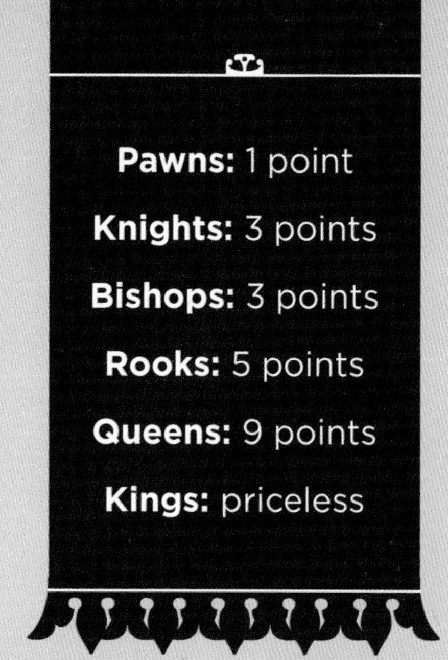

two squares, but after that they can inch forward only one square at a time. When they capture an enemy piece or pawn, they do it by moving *diagonally* forward into the square their opponent is occupying..

Pawns are considered as separate from your other pieces, and will be referred to in this way throughout the book. Since pawns are worth less in value (1 point), you'd almost always rather lose a pawn than a piece. Rarely will a rook, bishop, queen, or knight try to capture a pawn being defended by surrounding pawns or pieces.

They may not have a high material value, but pawns can be extremely useful in many ways, both on offense and defense. They also have a very effective secret weapon, which they keep hidden until the **endgame**, when the board is more open and the terrain less filled with dangers. Like any good soldier, they can be promoted! But more about that later . . . (See "Special Moves," page 28.)

ROOKS

The sturdy rook is a stout warrior, often designed to resemble a castle. The rook moves straight ahead for as many squares at a time as you want, so long as nothing is in its way. It can also move backward, all the way to its home rank if it's not blocked by another piece. Rooks can also move across the board from side to side along a rank, all the way from the **a** file to the **h** file. Like all the other pieces and pawns, rooks **capture**, or "take," by moving onto the square the enemy piece or pawn is occupying.

A castle is strong—sometimes nearly invincible. It is bursting with power, and made of sturdy stone. Such a fortress is not easily defeated, in life or in chess. With its wide range, and its ability to move quickly from one end of the board to the other, the rook is one of the most powerful pieces in the game—the second most powerful, in fact.

BISHOPS

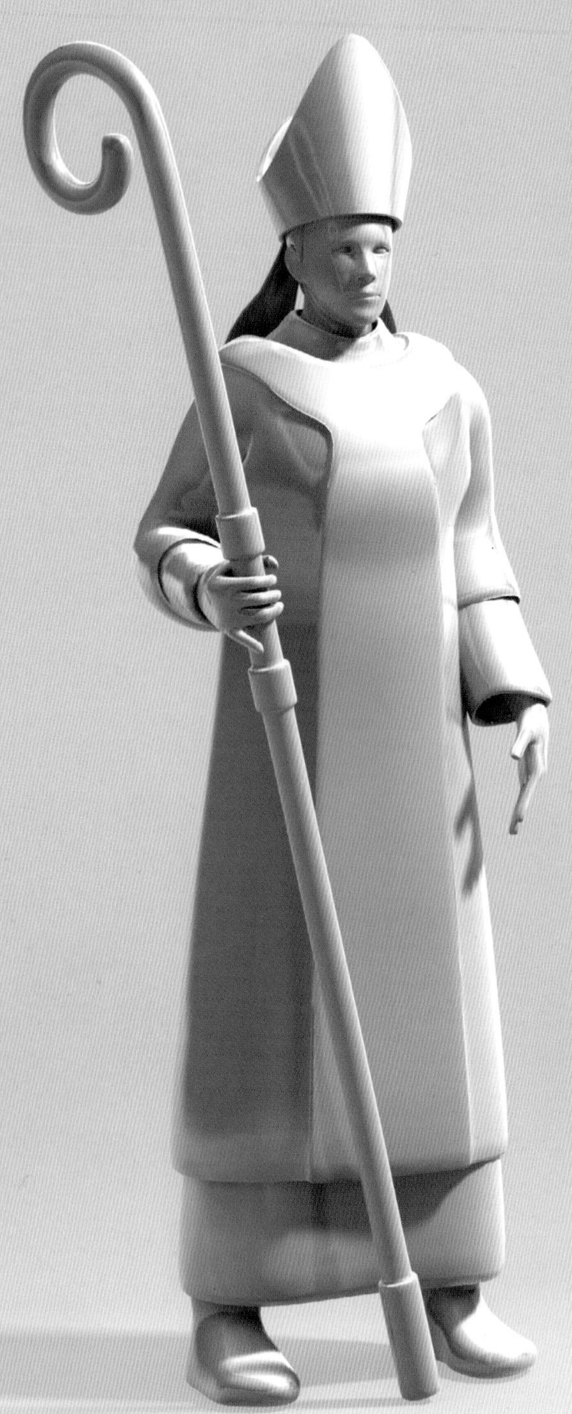

In real life, bishops are princes of the Church. They have a very clear vision of light and darkness, and will only go certain ways and not in others. Same with the bishops on the chessboard—you have two, but they will never cross paths. This is because one of your bishops lives only on the light squares, the other only on the dark.

The two bishops roam the diagonals of the chessboard, and can move as many as seven squares at a time. Between them, they can guard and menace an awful lot of territory. Without its twin, however, each bishop is far less powerful because it can only cover half the board at best—either the light or the dark squares, but not both. Your opponent can get around one bishop simply by moving to a square of the opposite shading. But when both your bishops are at work, covering both light and dark squares and projecting power over great distances, your opponent has no place to hide!

THE QUEEN

Throughout history, most queens have been sheltered in castles and palaces, hiding behind safe walls from any threat. But there have been quite a few queens—Elizabeth I of England and Cleopatra of Egypt come to mind—who have been as powerful and warlike as any king. The queen in chess is modeled after this type of monarch.

Indeed, the mighty queen is by far the most powerful piece on the board! She can move like a rook and bishop combined—forward, backward, and side to side like a rook, and on diagonals like a bishop—from one end of the board to the other.

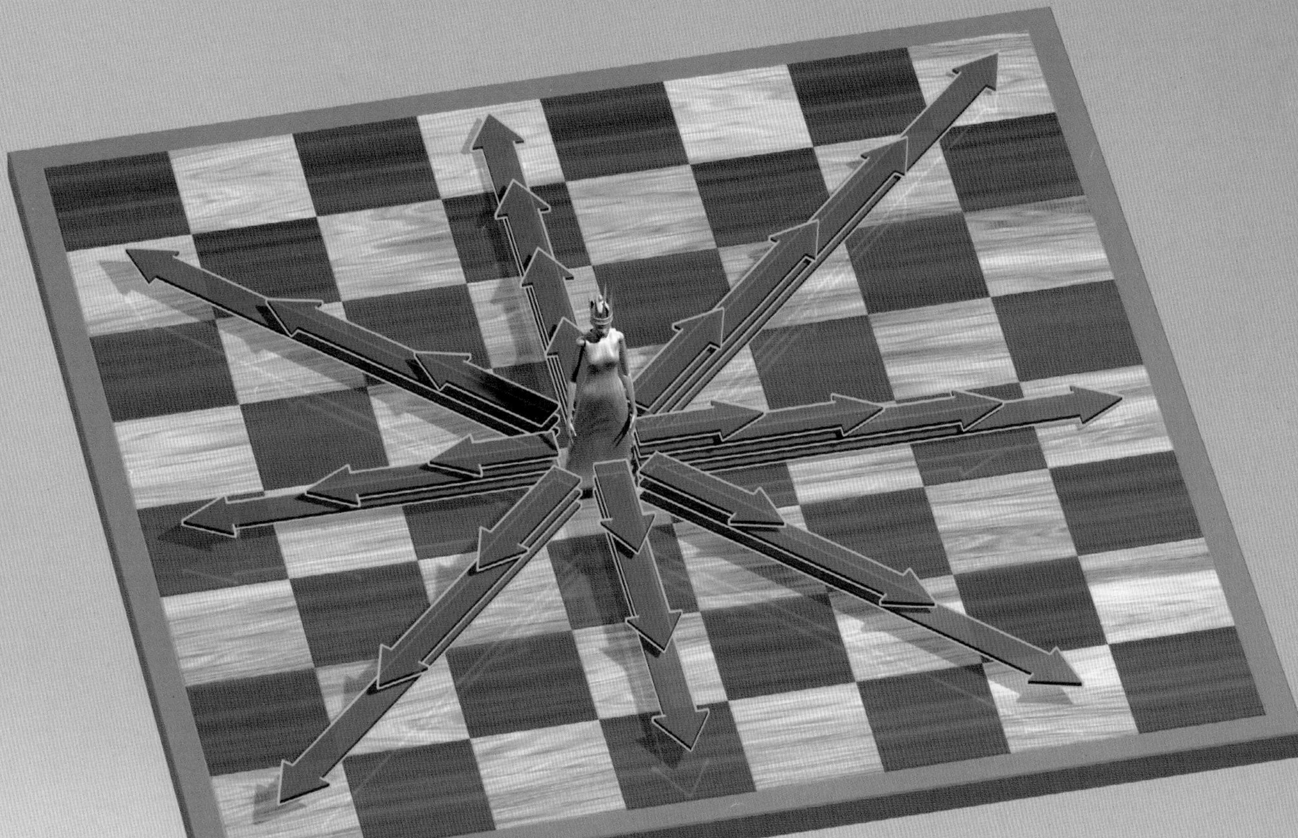

THE KING

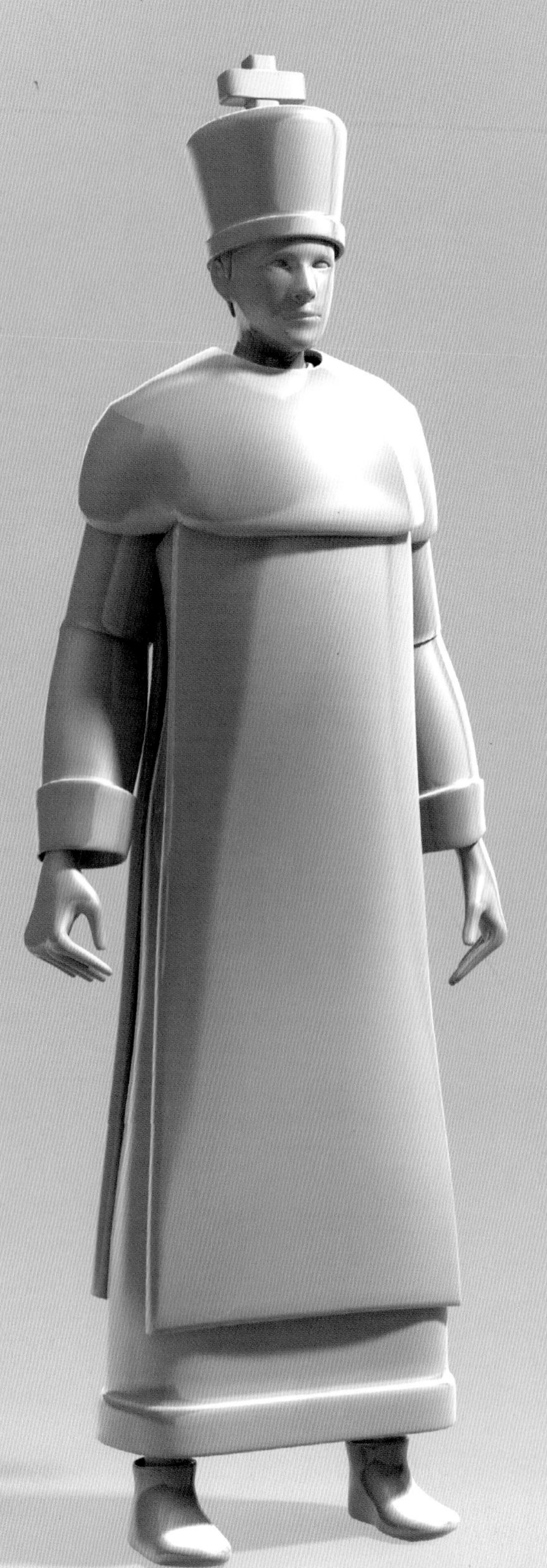

The king moves in all directions, just like the queen does, but much slower—unlike the queen, he can only cover one space at a time.

This certainly cuts down on the king's fighting value. Also, he cannot move himself to a square where he will be under attack and subject to capture (see "Victory and Defeat," page 24).

Still, the king is your most priceless treasure. Although he is not much of a fighter, he is worth more than any other piece in your army, for if the king is taken, the game is over. In fact, it's over even *before* the king can be taken—that's how precious he is. You can even think of *yourself* as the king, if you like, since in real life, the king controls the whole army. When the king is threatened, the army must throw everything into the fight to protect him, even sacrificing other pieces if necessary.

KNIGHTS

The knight—or "horse," as it is sometimes called because it is usually in that shape—can do things no other piece can. From their starting positions at b1, g1, b8, and g8, your two knights move in a basic "L" shape: two squares in one direction—*any* direction, other than diagonally—and one square to either side. Either part, the two- or the one-square advance, can come first.

Not even the mighty queen can jump over other pieces, or change directions mid-move. This makes the knight the most useful piece in chess for close fighting, where there aren't a lot of empty squares to maneuver in. The knight, because of its leaping ability, can get to those hard-to-reach squares and strike at the heart of the enemy's defense.

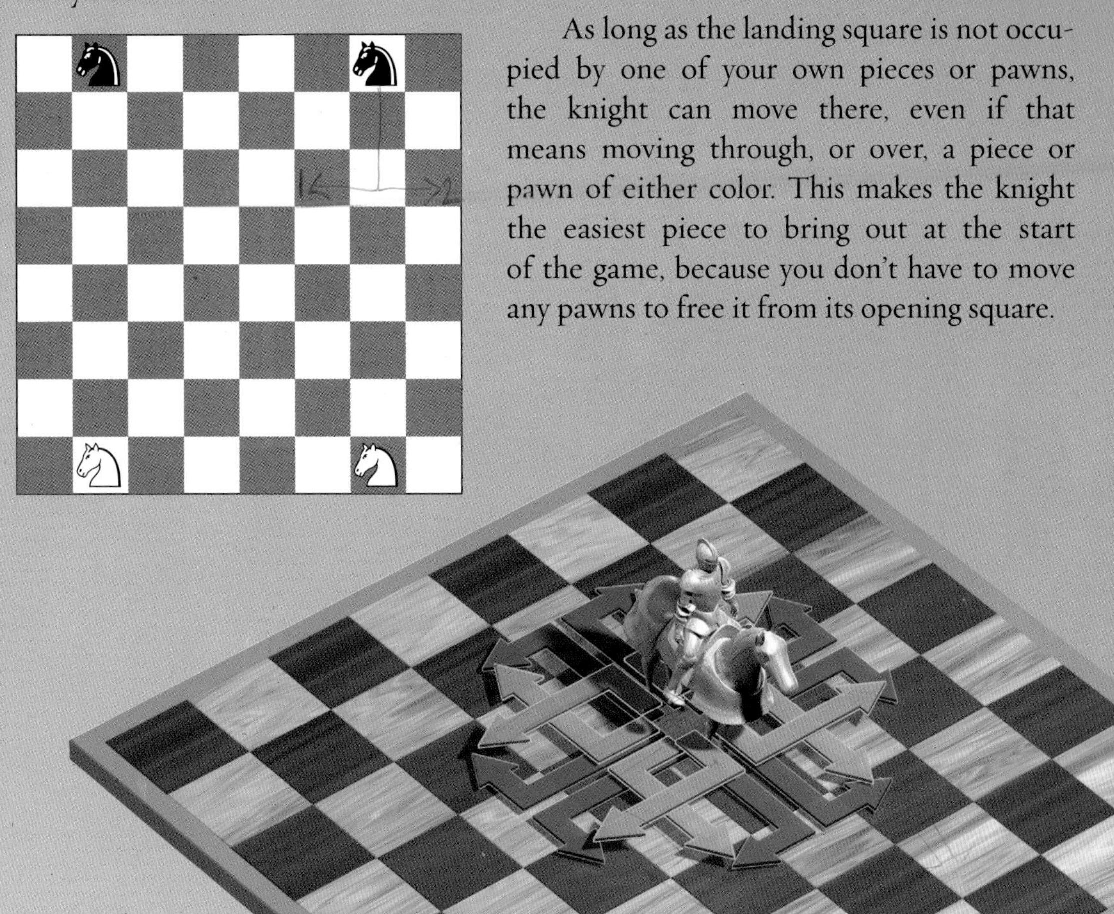

As long as the landing square is not occupied by one of your own pieces or pawns, the knight can move there, even if that means moving through, or over, a piece or pawn of either color. This makes the knight the easiest piece to bring out at the start of the game, because you don't have to move any pawns to free it from its opening square.

SET UP YOUR BOARD

Let's put it all together now, and muster the troops for battle!

At the beginning of any chess game, White's army occupies ranks 1 and 2, and Black occupies ranks 7 and 8.

Ranks 2 and 7 are for each side's pawns. Try lining them up now. Take out your chessboard, if you haven't already, and set up the pawns of both sides in their starting **positions**. White's pawns go on rank 2, all the way across the board from the a file to the h file. Black's go on rank 7, the same way. Now, let's put the various pieces behind them.

On ranks 1 and 8, rooks go in both corners (on the a and h files). Knights go next to them (on the b and g files), then bishops (on the c and f files). Kings begin the game on the e file, and queens on the d file. (See the diagram.)

Notice that, at the start of play, the queen stands by her king's side. You'll always remember which side to put her on because the queen always starts on a square of her own color: White queen on the light square, Black queen on the dark. The opposite is true for the king next to her. He starts each game on a square of the opposite color (to look at it another way, queens always start

at square d1 or d8; kings start on e1 and e8).

Bishops start the game by the sides of their king and queen, on squares c1, f1, c8, and f8. That's why they are sometimes called the "king's bishop" and the "queen's bishop." This is also true for knights and rooks on either **king side** or **queen side**. Pawns are referred to by the piece they stand in front of at the start of the game.

As you can see, it can feel a lot different playing White or Black. If you're Black, your king is on the left side of the board, whereas with White, the king is on the right side. It can be confusing, especially when trying to follow notation, but you'll soon get used to it.

CHESS NOTATION

Say you played a great game, and wanted to tell your friend all about it. You probably couldn't because it's difficult to remember what moves you made, let alone describe them to your friend. It's best to write them down so you can study and learn from them. That's why chess **notation** was invented—as long as 1,000 years ago, players were already recording their games!

Notation allows us not only to record our own games, but also to replay great games of the past and write out **chess problems** so that we can learn from them. Now that you know about pawns and pieces and how they move, it's time to get familiar with the "language" of chess.

As you learn to play by reading this book, you'll also learn the algebraic, or modern, system of chess notation. It's how we describe the moves of every game and exercise in this book. At first, there were many notation systems. In recent years, however, the algebraic system has become pretty much universal because it is the simplest way to describe chess moves. If you dig up an older chess book, you may find games recorded in an older system of notation, called "descriptive notation." Not to worry, though. You'll be able to figure it out. The old system may be clunkier than algebraic notation, but it's still easy to understand.

Algebraic chess notation is based on the system of numbers and letters for ranks, files, and diagonals already described in this book. Each piece, with the exception of the pawn, is represented by a letter:

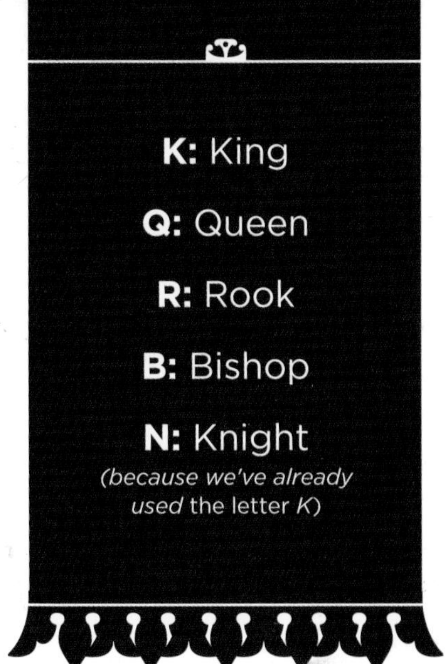

If no piece is mentioned before the square, it's a pawn move.

Pawns are normally described by the file (and sometimes rank) they occupy. Both players' kings' pawns would be described as "e" at the start of the game because that's the file they start on.

To describe a chess move, algebraic notation tells us the piece that is moved (unless it's a pawn, of course) and the square the piece moves to. If more than one piece or pawn of the same color can be moved to a particular square, the notation also tells us *which* piece or pawn is being moved, by giving us the file, and when necessary, the rank, the selected piece or pawn occupies *before* the move.

So that we can follow the progress of a game, moves are also numbered in order. White's and Black's first moves are considered move number one. They might be written this way, for instance:

1. e4...d5

Black's moves always have three dots in front of them. If you only wanted to write down Black's first move, you'd write **1. ...d5**

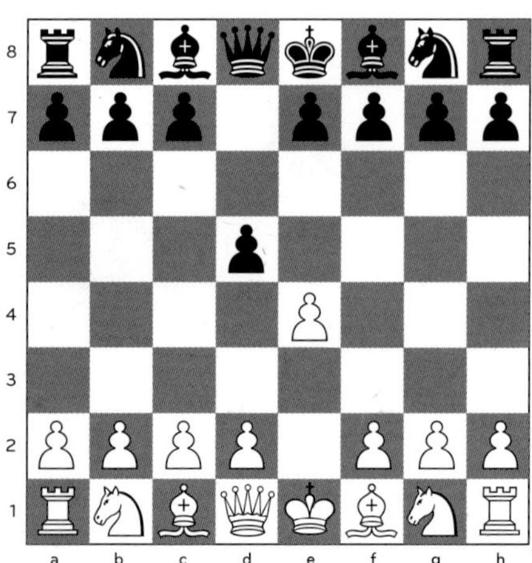

You'll notice that the notation doesn't use a P to indicate pawn. As noted before, for pawn moves, algebraic notation indicates only the square the pawn *moves to*. In our example, **1. e4** means that White's king's pawn moves from e2, its starting square, to e4. Remember that pawns can move two squares forward on their first move only. **1. ...d5** means that Black responds by moving his queen's pawn two squares forward, from d7, its starting square, to d5.

If White's king's pawn were now to take, or capture, Black's queen's pawn on move number two, it would be written:

2. exd5 (x is the symbol for "capture").

It can also be written more simply:

2. ed

We know there's a capture taking place because two pieces cannot occupy the same square at the same time. Since moving White's pawn from the e file to the d file can only be done by taking Black's pawn, **2. ed** is all the information you really need. Still, many times you'll see it written the first way, just to make things clearer.

In some cases, more detail is necessary, for instance, when two different pieces can move to one particular square.

Here, there are two pieces that can move to e4: White's king's pawn and his knight on c3. If it's the pawn we want to move, we write the move **e4**. If it's the knight we want to move, we write **Ne4**.

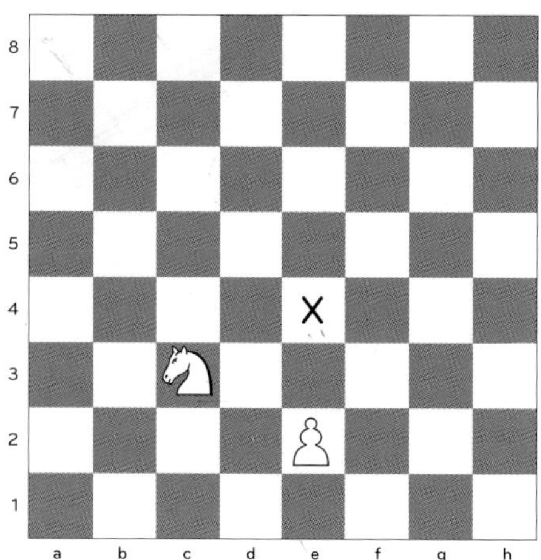

In this next diagram, there are two knights that can move to e4. We would write the move either **Nce4** or **Nde4**, depending upon which knight we wanted to move. Notice that the "c" or "d" denotes which file the knight was on *before* the move.

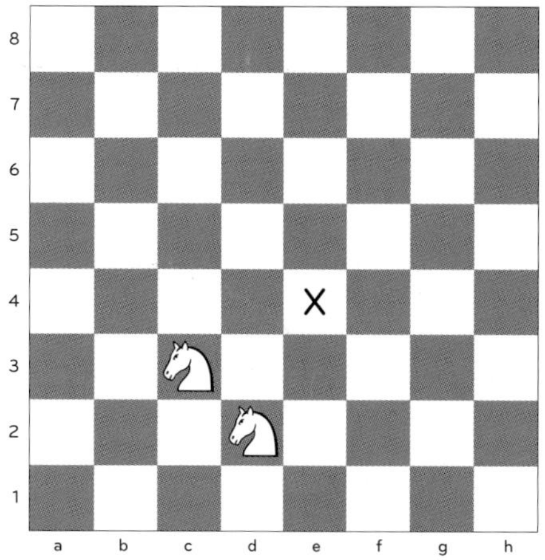

It may not be easy at first, but chess notation is very logical. When you get right down to it, so is the game itself! We know it's complicated. But once you get the hang of it, it'll be a piece of cake. Practice may not make perfect, but it sure does make things easier!

As we play through some standard chess **openings** (see pages 45-58) and games (see pages 61-78), you'll get to practice reading chess notation. When you start playing games on your own and you're more comfortable with it, you can start writing the moves down yourself so you can learn from them later. When you do, you'll want to note moves that are particularly good (!) or bad (?).

VICTORY AND DEFEAT

The object of the game of chess is simple—to **checkmate** your opponent. That does not mean, as in so many video games, simply to kill enemies until there are none left.

In chess, it never comes to that. A player is checkmated when his king is under attack ("in **check**"), has no means of escape or defense, and will inevitably be captured with the attacker's next move.

Notice we use the word "captured," or "taken," not "killed." In chess, there is far too much honor and nobility to shed blood—even *virtual* blood—but that doesn't make the combat any less mortal, or the outcome any less final!

When you place your opponent's king under direct **attack**, he is said to be "in check" (notation symbol **+**). He must move his king to safety, block the attack with one of his other pieces, or else capture the attacking piece or pawn with one of his own. A check is dangerous, but not fatal.

RULE #1: PROTECT YOUR KING AT ALL COSTS!
Never leave him undefended or open to attack. And always make sure he has an escape route.

In this diagram, Black's king is in check. He can escape the attack by moving his king to d8 or f8. He can block the check by moving his queen to e7. Or he can capture the attacking queen with his own queen by Qe6. This position is highly unlikely in a real chess game, but it serves to show the three ways out of check.

Sometimes, though, those three ways of escape are not all available to a player.

But when a player is checkmated, or as we often say, **mated** (notation symbol **#**), his defeat is total. There is no escape—the game is over. No wonder so many players "resign," giving up the fight, when they realize they cannot avoid being checkmated. And no wonder the word "checkmate" has found its way into everyday language.

In **tournaments**, players can also lose a game by forfeit. Forfeits happen when one player fails to make a move before his time runs out. That's right—in tournaments, there's a time limit on the players! We'll go into that more in the section on tournament chess (page 89).

"In life, unlike chess, the game continues after checkmate."
—*Isaac Asimov, American writer*

"Diplomacy is a game of chess in which the nations are checkmated."
—*Karl Kraus, Austrian writer*

TIE GAME

Most chess games end when one player wins and the other loses, but sometimes *neither* player wins.

A DRAW CAN HAPPEN

- by agreement. One player offers a **draw**, and the other accepts. The players shake hands, and it's over. It's as simple as that. When both players feel there's no likelihood of either side winning, there's not much sense in going on with the game. Most draws happen this way.

- by attrition, when neither player has enough pieces and pawns left to checkmate the other. For example, a king plus a knight or bishop, but no pawns, cannot checkmate a lone king. By rule, this type of situation results in a draw.

- by three-fold repetition of a position. The same position is returned to for the third time in a game, and either player points it out. This does not mean that both players have to make the same six (back and forth) moves in a row, but it most often happens that way, and the declared draw keeps the game from going on forever with no outcome.

- by 50-move rule. If the players each make 50 moves without capturing a piece or moving a pawn, and one player points this out, the game is automatically drawn. This almost never happens outside of tournaments.

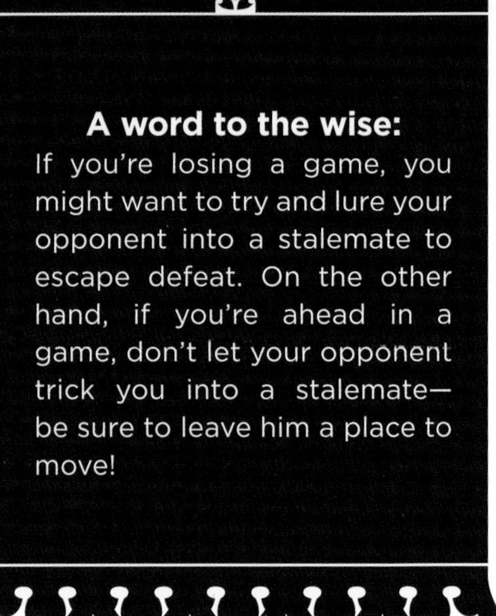

A word to the wise:
If you're losing a game, you might want to try and lure your opponent into a stalemate to escape defeat. On the other hand, if you're ahead in a game, don't let your opponent trick you into a stalemate—be sure to leave him a place to move!

- by arriving at a **stalemate**, which is more like a tie than a draw. This happens when a player is not in check, but cannot make a legal move because all his or her pieces are blocked from moving.

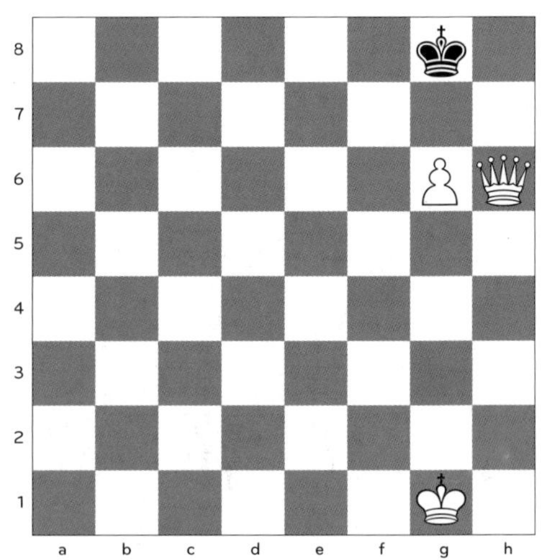

Notice that Black's king cannot move without putting himself in check, which would be an illegal move.

CHESS PROBLEM: "CHECK, CHECKMATE, OR STALEMATE"

Here is a fun and valuable chess problem for you to try and solve. For each of the four diagrams below, figure out whether the position is check, checkmate, or stalemate:

(Turn to page 113 for the answers.)

1.

2.

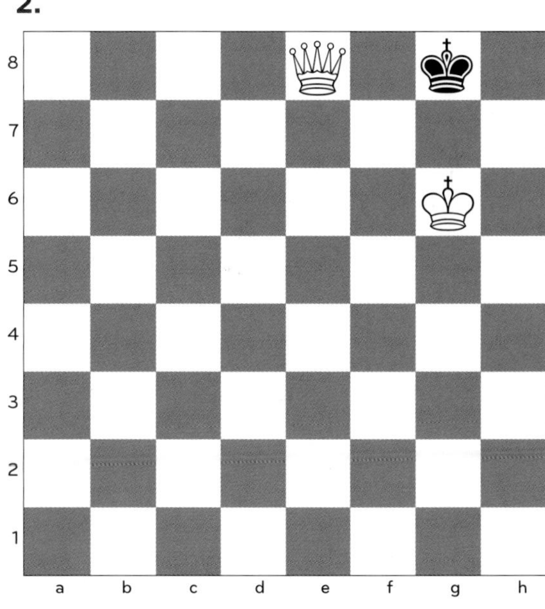

3.

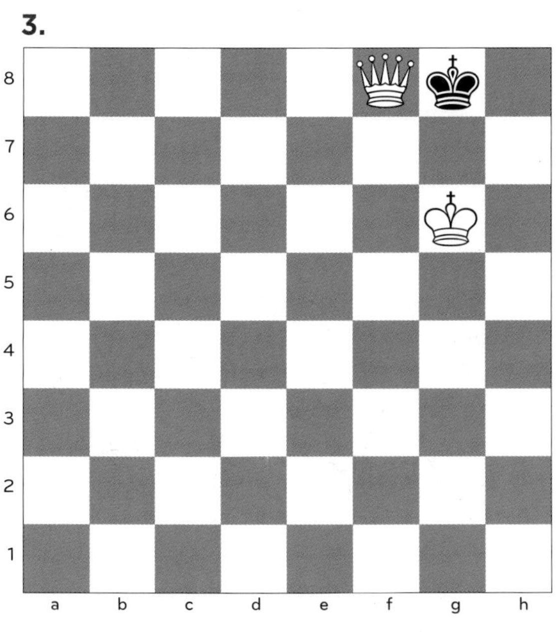

4.

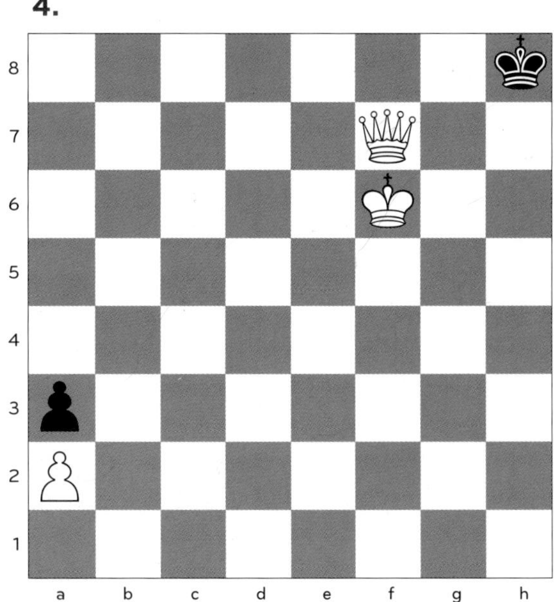

SPECIAL MOVES

Before we move on to playing actual games, there are three special moves you need to know about.

PAWN PROMOTION

If a pawn, by moving forward square by square, finally reaches the last rank (rank 1 for a Black pawn or rank 8 for a White pawn), it transforms like a fairy-tale frog kissed by a princess! When the lowly pawn reaches the last rank safely, it can become any piece you choose other than a king. Of course, you'll almost always want to make it a second queen since she's the most powerful. The queen can make all the moves of the other pieces, and more, except for the unique way a knight moves. That's why sometimes you'll choose to promote your pawn to a knight instead, especially if, as a knight, it is in position to help checkmate the opposing king!

If your queen is still on the board when you promote your pawn to a second queen, you can use a captured rook, placing it upside down to represent the new queen. Lucky thing rooks will stand up in the upside-down position. If both your rooks are still on the board, use a coin or something else to represent your new queen—be creative!

In addition to pawn promotion, there are two other special moves to know about. The first one is used very rarely; the second occurs in almost every chess game:

EN PASSANT

En passant ("e.p." in algebraic notation), French for "in passing," refers to a unique way that one pawn can capture another. If a pawn's first move is an advance of two squares, it may then be taken by an enemy pawn standing next to it, which then moves into the square *behind* the captured pawn.

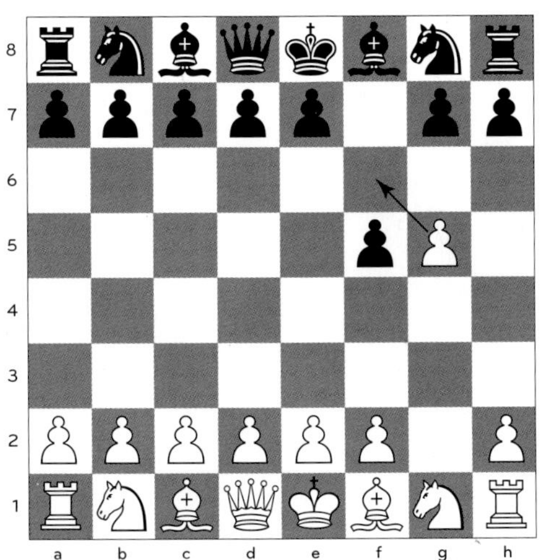

In the diagram, Black's pawn has moved from f7 to f5. The White pawn on g5 can then take the Black pawn en passant by moving to f6. The capturing player must do this at the first opportunity, and cannot wait to make this move later. This move is rare, but effective, especially since your opponent may have forgotten that en passant exists!

CASTLING

The third special move is called **castling**, which involves the king and the rook. Castling is a wonderful way to get your king to a safe spot on the board, while at the same time freeing your rook to take part in the action. It's such a special move that you only get to do it once in a game!

Castling is the only move in chess that breaks three rules at once:

- It is the only move in chess that involves two pieces moving at once.
- It is the only move where the king can move more than one square at once.
- It is the only move where pieces other than the knight get to jump over each other.

At the beginning of the game, the king sits in the center of the back rank—a vulnerable spot. He can be attacked from the front, or from either side.

One sensible defensive **strategy** is to move him over to one side of the board, away from the central file he occupies and from the furious action that usually takes place there. Here, in the corner, he can be attacked only from two directions instead of three.

You can castle either to the king side or the queen side of the board, always on your back rank. In king-side castling, the king moves from the e file to the g file, and the rook moves from the h file to the f file. This all happens in one move:

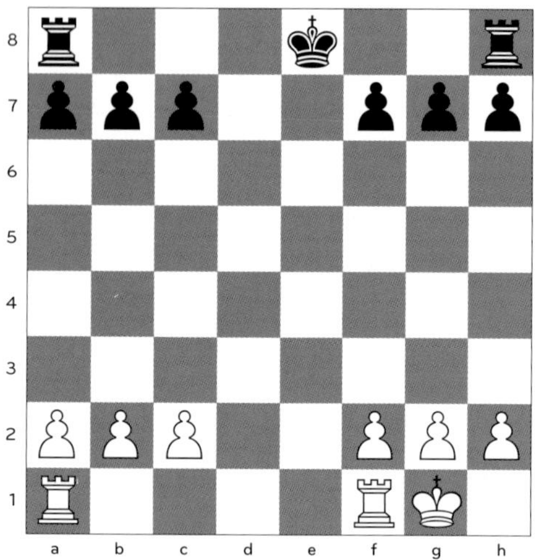

In queen-side castling, it's just the opposite. The king moves two spaces, from the e file to the c file, and the rook jumps over him, moving three spaces in this case, from the a file to the d file.

When castling, you'll want to make sure the king is protected by a wall of pawns, and perhaps some other pieces, too. Be sure to leave him an escape square, or **luft**, at some point, as well, so he can't be trapped back there in a sudden ambush! Later on, we'll go into the various ways to create this escape square for the king.

Castling early is a great way to protect your king and get your rook into the battle, but you can't do it if there are pieces in the way. In addition, it has to be the first move for both your king and your rook. You can't castle if your king is in check, if he would have to move through a check to get to his new space on the board, or if the square the king would move to is under attack, as shown in the diagram below.

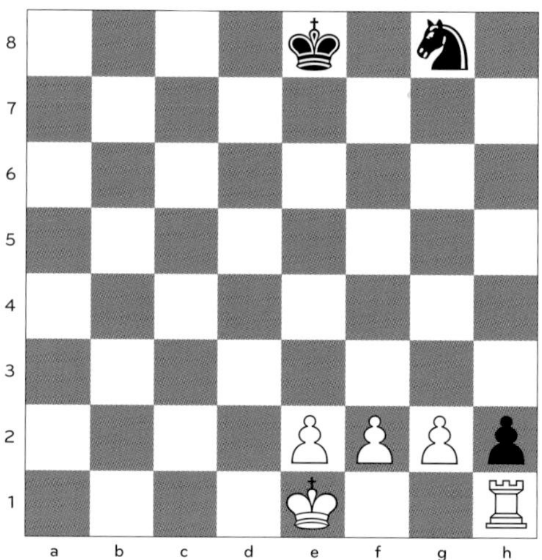

In chess notation, king-side castling is written like this: **0-0**. Queen-side castling is written: **0-0-0**. We know that it seems weird. But just trust us and go with it—we promise, you'll find castling to be extremely useful!

TOUCH MOVE RULE

When you're first starting out at chess, and you're playing someone more experienced, that person may let you take back a bad move you've just made. That's fine if it helps you learn the game faster. But when you start playing games *for real*, whether it's just a friendly **match** or a world chess championship, the **touch-move** rule always applies.

Once you've touched a piece, you have to move that piece (if it is a legal move). Once you've moved that piece to a square and let go of it, the move is set in stone—you can't take it back. If you pick up one of your pieces and touch an enemy piece with it, you must use your piece to capture that enemy piece or pawn (if it's legal).

So it's best to remember simply to keep your hands off the pieces until you're absolutely sure which move you want to make!

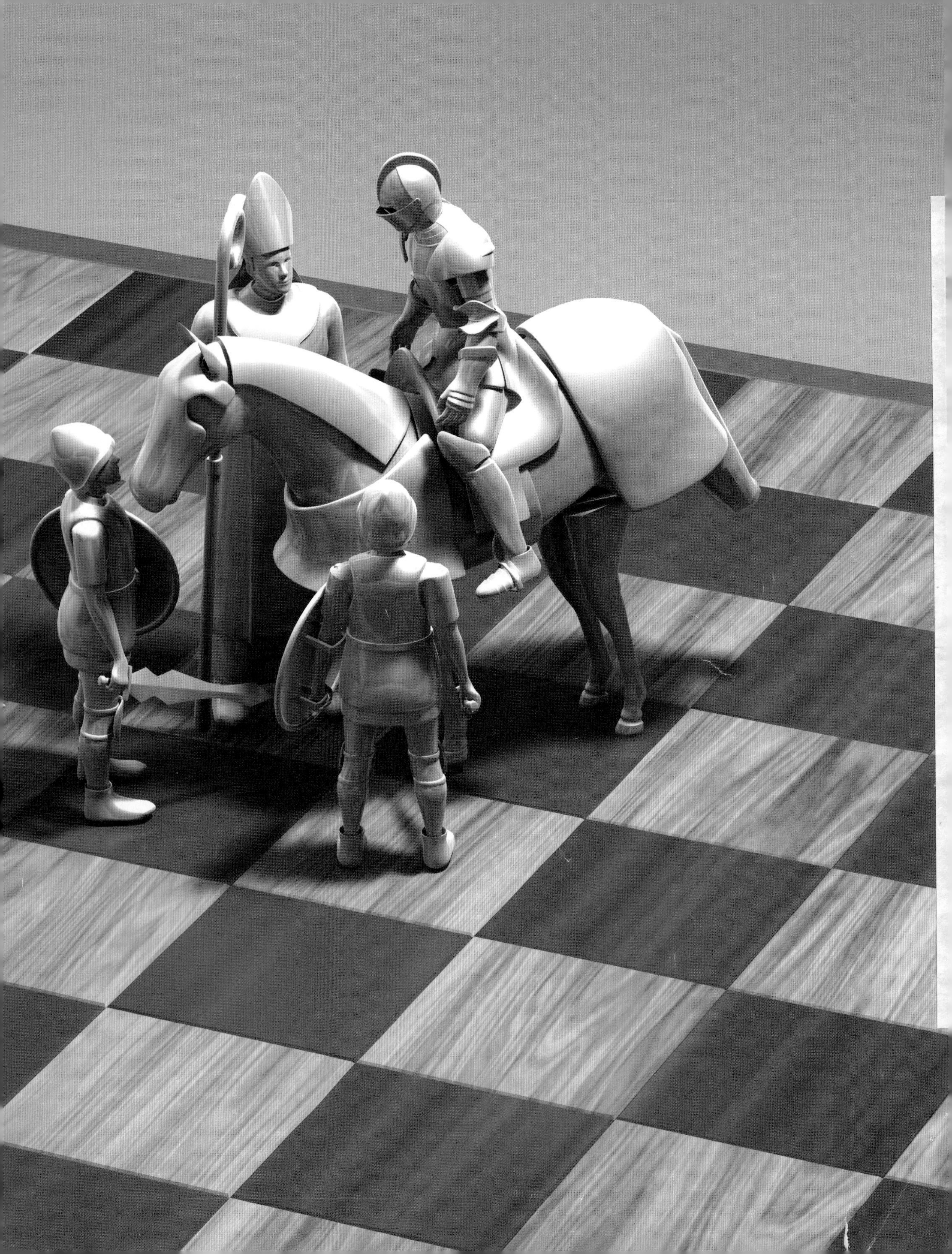

CHAPTER TWO

BASIC PRINCIPLES

Winning at chess depends on staying ahead of your opponent, but there's more than one way to get ahead! You can capture pawns and pieces to achieve a material advantage. You can get to a key square first, forcing the enemy into defending himself instead of developing his pieces or attacking you, which, if you think about it, is a time advantage. Or, you can gain an advantage in position, allowing you to attack your opponent's weaknesses while still maintaining a solid defense.

A **sacrifice** is when you allow a pawn or piece to be captured for a good reason, such as the opportunity to launch an unstoppable attack. For instance, you might let one of your bishops be captured without gaining any enemy pieces, but instead you use your move to place your queen close to the enemy king in order to attack it.

Capturing is simply the act of taking an enemy pawn or piece off the board. For example, your rook moves forward to take an enemy knight and removes it from the board.

A **trade** is when one piece or pawn is captured at the expense of one of equal value. For example, you capture an enemy pawn but lose a pawn of your own.

Exchange can mean two things: There is the verb, to exchange, and the noun, the exchange. The verb "to exchange" is to give up pawns, pieces, or both, and be able to capture enemy pawns, pieces, or both on the following move. Exchanging can mean that material of equal value on opposing sides is lost. It can also mean that one side loses more material than the other. To put it more clearly, a trade is always an exchange but an exchange is not always a trade.

The noun "exchange" means that one side has given up a bishop or knight for an enemy rook. If, for instance, White captures Black's rook with his knight, then has that knight captured in return, White is then said to be "up the exchange," because he has gained an advantage in material.

STRATEGY—THE KEY TO WINNING CHESS

GAINING THE MATERIAL EDGE

Material advantage—having more pieces and pawns than your opponent—is a good thing. Usually, the player with the most material at the end of the game winds up winning, but not always!

If your position is better, or if you get, and keep, the **initiative** (in other words, the time advantage), your opponent's material advantage alone won't win him the game. Often, good players successfully **sacrifice** material to gain a big advantage in position or initiative.

But, at first, the main thing to remember is that you want to capture more pieces and pawns than you give up.

Again, here is the chart showing the relative value of pawns and pieces:

Pawns	=	1 point
Knights	=	3 points
Bishops	=	3 points
Rooks	=	5 points
Queens	=	9 points
Kings	=	priceless

So why are rooks and queens worth more than either knights or bishops? For one thing, they can project their power from the safe, faraway corners of the board. The center is dangerous, yet that's where knights and bishops are most useful.

For another thing, in the **endgame**, a king and a rook (or queen) alone can checkmate the opponent's king. A king and either a bishop or knight need at least one pawn to help them. In other words, you can checkmate the enemy king with only your own king and a **major piece**, but not with only your king and a **minor piece**. Queens and rooks are most valuable to you in the endgame, when it *really* counts.

So what's the bottom line on material? You've got to do the math! If, for instance, you're capturing a queen but losing your rook in exchange, that's a very good deal. On the other hand, is exchanging a rook for a bishop a good deal for you? Not by the math—no way!

As long as your opponent loses more points than you do, it's a good exchange for you—at least, in terms of material value. Of course, if giving up the material edge helps you unleash a powerful attack, it might be worth the sacrifice! (See "The Art of Sacrifice," page 72.)

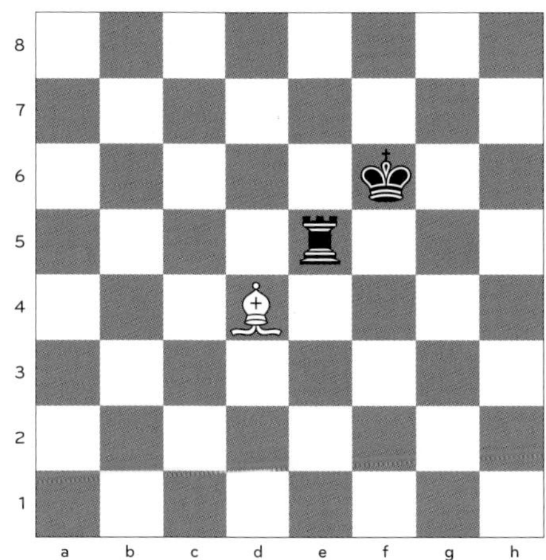

Notice that bishops and knights are each worth three points. You already know they do very different jobs. Deciding whether to exchange a bishop for a knight can be a tough call. Bishops are good long-range weapons, especially on a more open board, because they can move more freely. They can also sometimes strike faster, as in a "discovered check" (see page 42).

Here, moving the rook away from square e5 means the bishop on d4 is checking Black's king! A knight can't be used for a discovered check. But knights can maneuver on squares of both colors, while each bishop is limited to half the squares on the board. And knights can jump over obstacles, making them more useful in the more cluttered positions typical of the **middle game**.

Having two bishops in the more wide-open endgame has proven over time to be particularly powerful because between them, on an open board, they can cover every square on the board. Having two knights is also generally a stronger position than having one bishop and one knight, partly because they can protect one another—something a knight and a bishop together cannot do.

Each piece may be worth the same as three pawns, but which is better? Well, that depends on which pieces you and your opponent have left and what the game situation demands. Some chess experts say a bishop is worth an extra $1/4$ or $1/2$ point than a knight. But

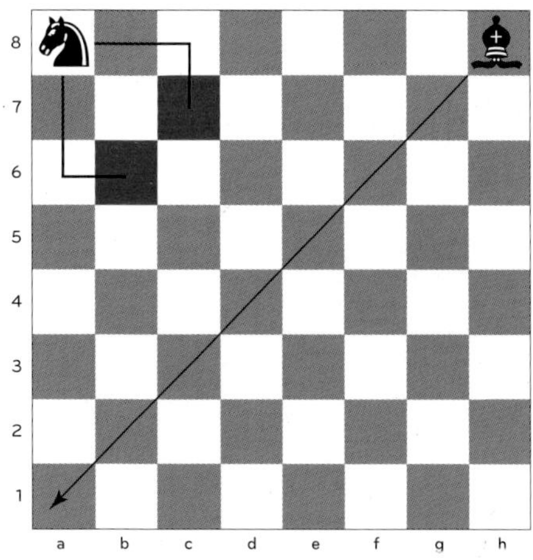

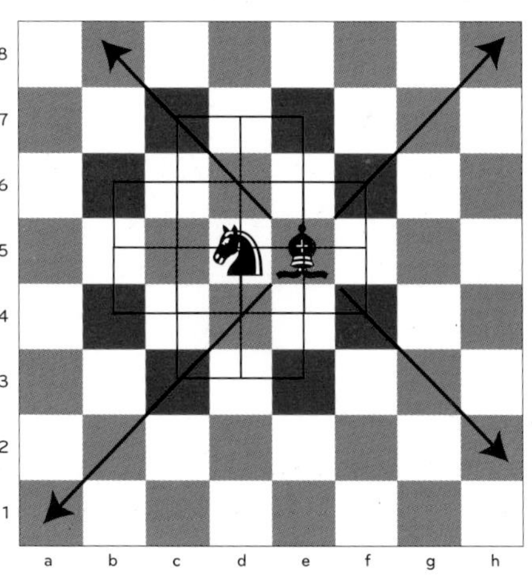

in the end, it's a pretty close call—it really comes down to how well you play with the pieces you've got!

GETTING—AND KEEPING—THE INITIATIVE

In any game of chess, White always moves first. That's just the way chess has come down to us through the ages. You might think that gives White an advantage, and you'd be right. White wins around 55 percent of the time, Black only about 45 percent. That's why in chess matches of more than one game the opponents always alternate playing White and Black.

Since White goes first, he starts the game with the **initiative**. Black, at least in the opening, mostly plays catch-up until White makes a mistake and surrenders one move's worth of time, or a **tempo**. White can lose a tempo by making outright mistakes (see "Fool's Mate," page 39) or simply by playing unnecessary moves that add nothing to the development of his position.

As long as your move makes your opponent do something to prevent your next move, he has no time to execute his own plans! Whichever side you're playing, it's vital to make every move count—and it's even better when you find a move that accomplishes two or more goals at once! For instance, if you advance a piece or pawn to a central square, and threaten an enemy piece or pawn at the same time, your opponent can only react to one problem or the other.

Ask yourself before you make a move, "Is this move going to help me? How? Am I developing my position by advancing my pieces to key squares? Fortifying my defense? Preparing an attack?" Make sure you know why you're making a move!

DOMINATING THE BOARD

Gaining positional advantage, or controlling the board, is another important point when it comes to winning at chess. When you control most of the board, you're almost certain to come out on top. To win the positional game, you start by advancing your pawns and pieces, or **developing** them, and thereby gain control of the center of the board. Doing this will give you room to maneuver your pieces, and will keep your opponent on the defensive. That doesn't mean you can't maneuver along the sides, or **flanks**, of the board, but the center will always be more important to control.

To gain control of the center directly, start the game by getting your central pawns out there, supporting one another and making room for your pieces to operate. Then bring out the knights to support the pawns and take aim at the four central squares: d4, d5, e4, and e5. It's also possible to exert control on the central squares indirectly, from a distance, for instance, with a **fianchetto** of your bishop (see page 56). A fianchetto is when you position one of your bishops to attack the center squares of the chessboard from the sides, or flanks, of the board, keeping that piece out of danger. We'll look at indirect control of the center when we study some typical openings.

RULE #2: THE BEST DEFENSE IS A GOOD OFFENSE

As long as you are on the attack, you have the initiative. And as long as you have the initiative, your opponent will find it almost impossible to get an attack of his own under way. Just be sure you can keep up your attack and not hand back the initiative, because in attacking, it's easy to bring yourself out of position and vulnerable to counterattack! Ask yourself, "If I attack, how will my opponent defend himself? Does he have a way to counterattack? And do I have pieces and pawns in reserve to help keep up the attack once I've started it, or will I have to retreat?"

Pawns can be your shock troops if you succeed in developing them early. By forming a defensive wall, they can also serve to block enemy pieces and pawns—even heavy pieces—from taking part in the action. This is done by placing them in diagonal or zigzag (that is, a3, b2, c3, d4, e3, f4, etc.) formation, so that if any pawn is taken, another can capture the enemy piece that did the taking.

After the pawns, knights and bishops are usually the first pieces to advance, the first to attack, and the first pieces lost in battle. They are called "minor pieces" because you can't win a game with just one of them and your king alone.

Once you've gained the upper hand in the center of the board, and made sure your king is safe, you'll be able to use your mobility to launch an attack on your opponent, who will be suffering from cramped quarters because you've taken over all the maneuvering room on the battlefield! This is the time to bring your major pieces—your rook and queen—into the battle.

Rooks do especially well when they're lined up on an **open file**, or one with no pawns blocking the rook's path. Two rooks, or a rook and a queen, lined up on an open file or rank are a devastating **combination** known as a battery, as in battering ram, the ancient military device used to break down walls and doors. Your opponent has to devote a lot of time and energy to defend against this double threat because if one of your rooks is captured, your other rook can then capture the attacking piece or pawn. Rooks are deadly when used in pairs, either on the same rank or on the same file. Look at all the spaces these two rooks can cover between them:

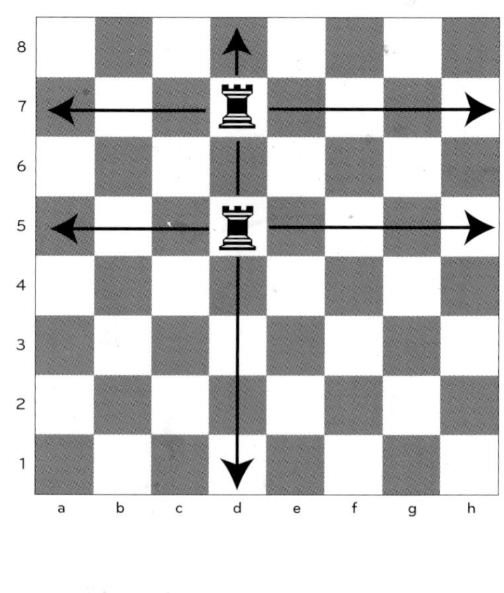

TWO QUICK MATES

What follows are two fine examples of what can happen to a chess player who disregards the basic principles we've just gone over:

FOOL'S MATE

Here is the notated version of **Fool's Mate**. It's called that because it only takes White two moves to totally blow the game! This is the shortest possible chess game, and the quickest possible checkmate. See if you can use the notation to follow the action:

1. **f3...e5**
2. **g4...Qh4#—checkmate!**

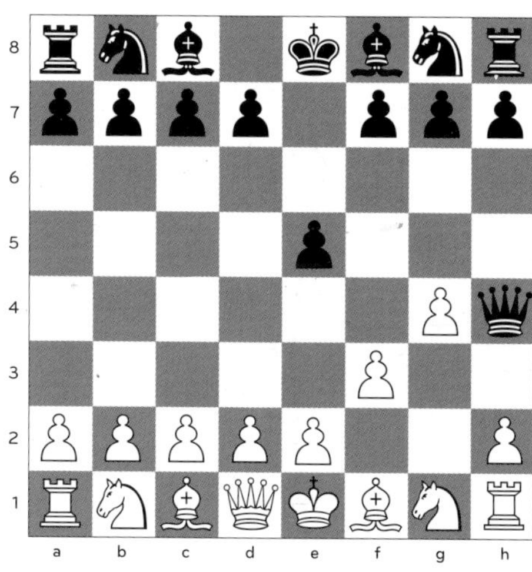

Did you spot the "mate" coming? What mistake did White make? That's right—he broke rule #1! White left his king totally at the mercy of Black's queen.

Don't be like this fool! Protect your king at all costs!

ORDER OF DEVELOPMENT

Here's a little list to help you remember the general rules of pawn and piece development. Use it more as a flexible guide than as an absolute rule:

1. Pawns to the center
2. Knights to the center
3. Bishops to the center
4. Castle
5. Develop your **major pieces** (queen and rooks)

SCHOLAR'S MATE

Scholar's Mate is the most common quick checkmate. Here's how it goes:

1. **e4...e5** (So far, so good.)
2. **Bc4...Nc6**

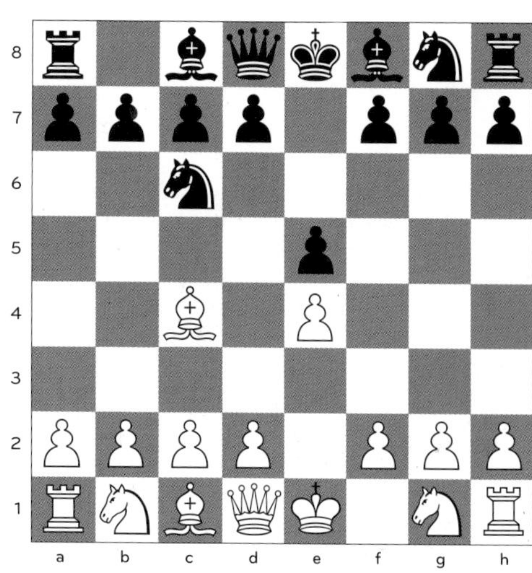

White develops his bishop before his knight, whereas Black sticks with the basics and develops his knight first.

3. Qh5...

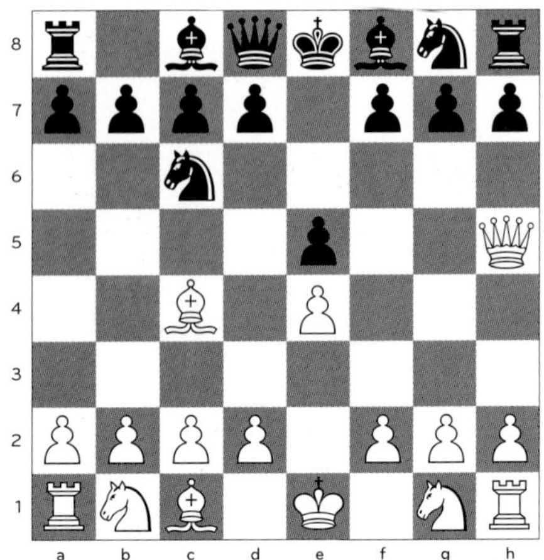

It's usually not a good idea to bring the queen so far out this early in the game. If your opponent develops his queen early, it is probably because he wants to deliver Scholar's Mate, or the "four-move checkmate." You can prevent this from happening. Any time you see your opponent developing his queen early, tell yourself two things. First: "Look out!" Your opponent is probably trying for Scholar's Mate. Second: "Be happy." This early queen move should put your opponent in a vulnerable position, so take advantage. But, be careful! Check out the next foolish move by Black:

3. ...Nf6??

Rather than defending the f7 pawn, which is still under attack by White's bishop for the second move in a row, black tries to attack the white queen too quickly! This seals his fate. However, black could have played **3. ...g6**, which

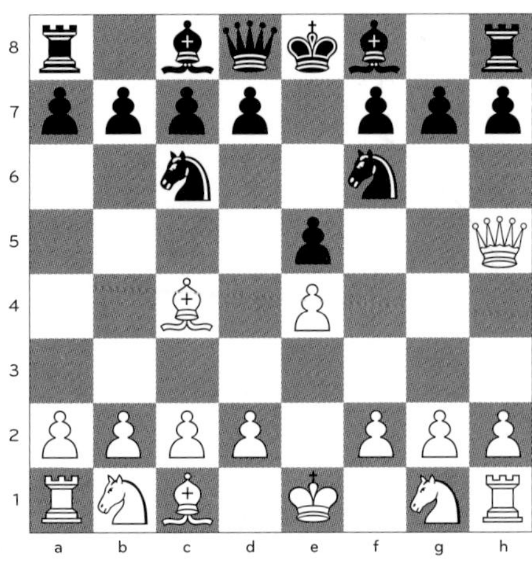

stops the checkmate in move #4, and attacks the queen.

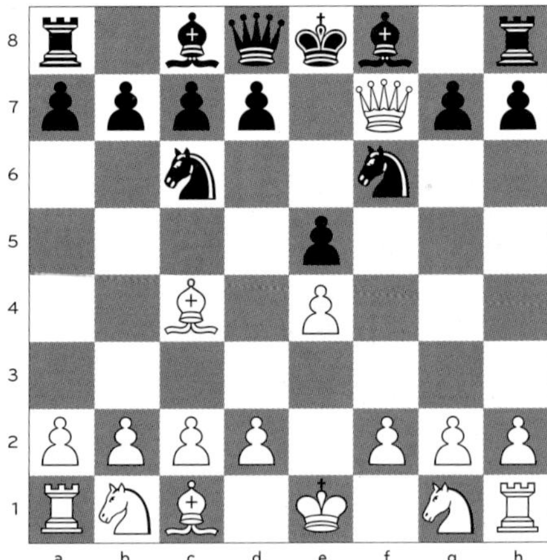

4. Qxf7#!!

This checkmate has occurred thousands of times and will probably occur thousands more times. It's important to know how to do the Scholar's Checkmate, but it's more important to know how to prevent it from happening to you!

Maybe one day you too will be able to trap your opponent like this. How cool would that be? But most games are much longer and more complicated, so don't expect every game to end so fast!

TACTICS AND OTHER SHARP THINGS

FORKS

A **fork** is an attack by one player on two or more enemy pieces or pawns. The fork is one of the best ways to gain the material edge. In the diagram here, Black's knight is forking White's queen and rook. White can save one piece, but not the other. Of course, he will choose to save the queen, which is worth more than the rook. Either way, even if White captures his knight in return, Black comes out ahead in the exchange.

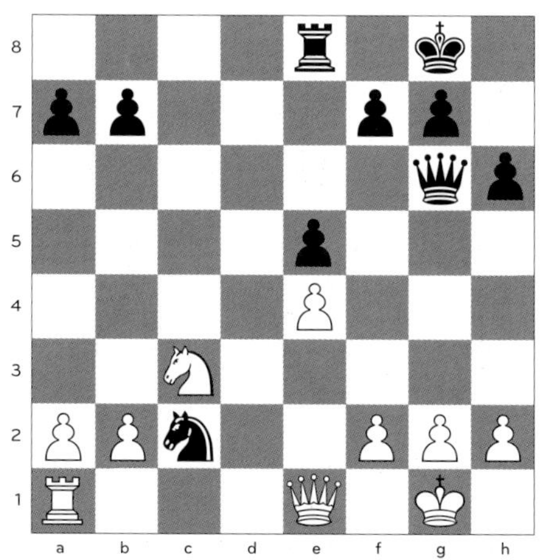

As a player on offense, you should be watching for opportunities to fork your opponent's pieces. On the other hand, never put your own pieces in position to be forked!

Here, the fork includes a check. When the Black king moves, as he must to avoid check from White's knight, the knight will capture Black's queen!

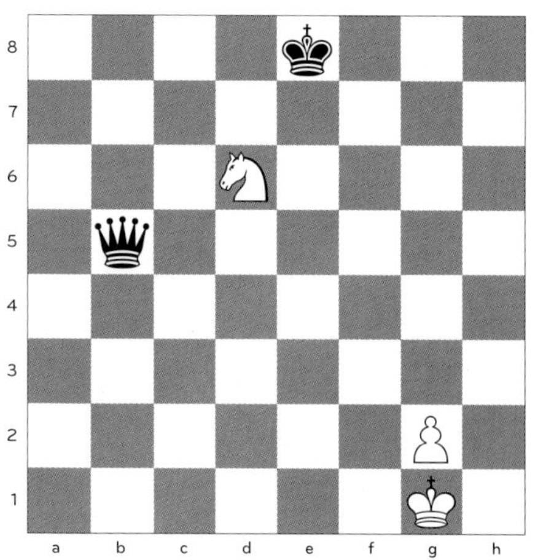

PINS

A **pin** happens when one player is forcing the other to leave one of his pawns or pieces in place to protect another, more valuable piece. He cannot move the protecting pawn or piece without exposing the piece behind it to capture.

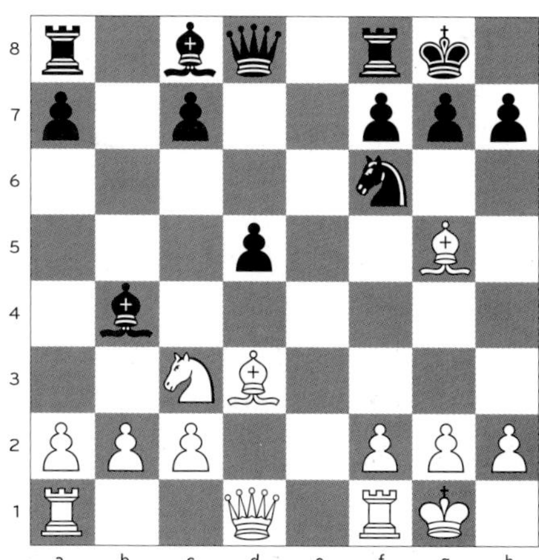

In the diagram above, White's bishop has pinned Black's knight. If the knight moves, Black's queen can be captured! In the next diagram, Black's rook has pinned White's queen. The queen cannot move because the king would be exposed to capture.

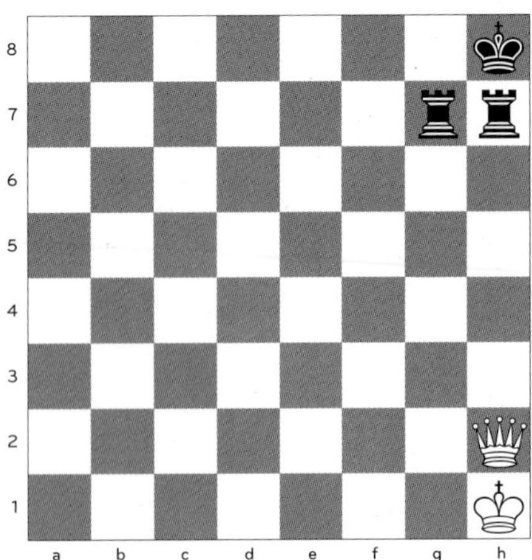

SKEWERS

The opposite of a pin, **skewering** your opponent means threatening one of her pieces and forcing it to move; then, when it does, capturing another, less valuable piece or pawn that was positioned behind the one that moved.

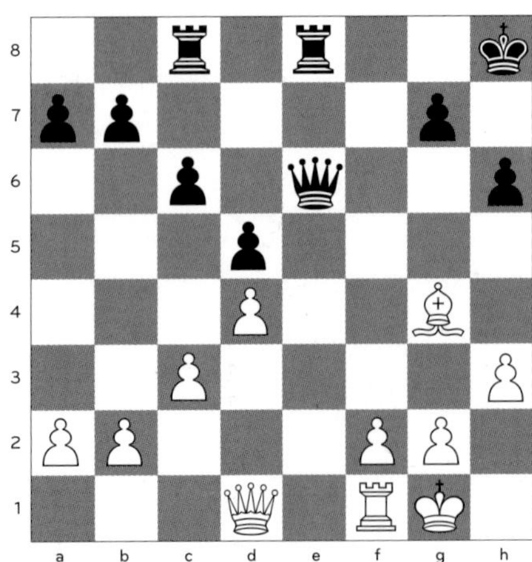

Here, White's bishop will take Black's rook once Black's queen is out of the way. Of course, Black could leave his queen in place and subject to capture, but that would be foolish, since the queen is worth much more than the rook.

DISCOVERED CHECK

Discovered check happens when one player moves one of his pieces out of the way of another behind it, which then is able to attack the enemy king. Here, White's knight moves from d5 to b4, putting Black's king in check with White's bishop on c4.

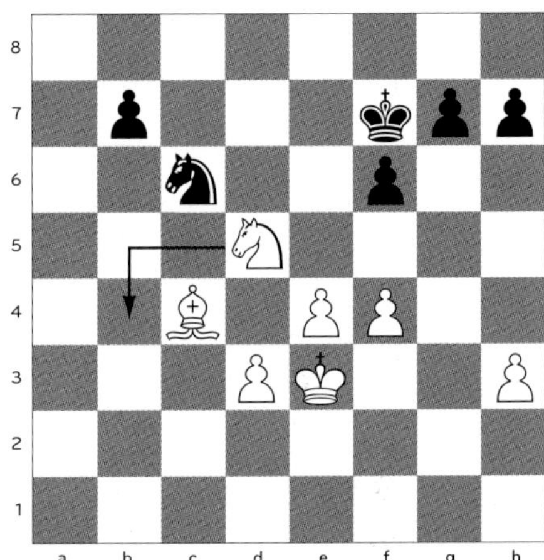

When the moving piece also checks the enemy king, it's not only a discovered check; it's also a **double check**! Here, Black's rook moves to d8, checking White's king, and also discovering a check by Black's bishop on c5.

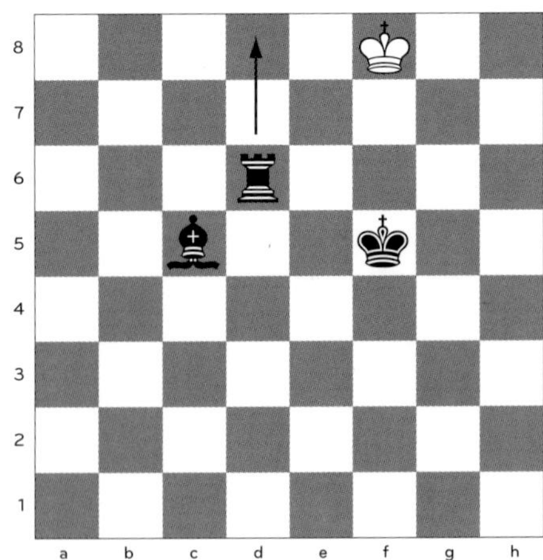

DISCOVERED ATTACKS

A **discovered attack** is the same as a discovered check, but without the check. Here, for instance, it's White's queen that comes under attack by a lesser piece—Black's bishop—when Black's knight moves out of the way.

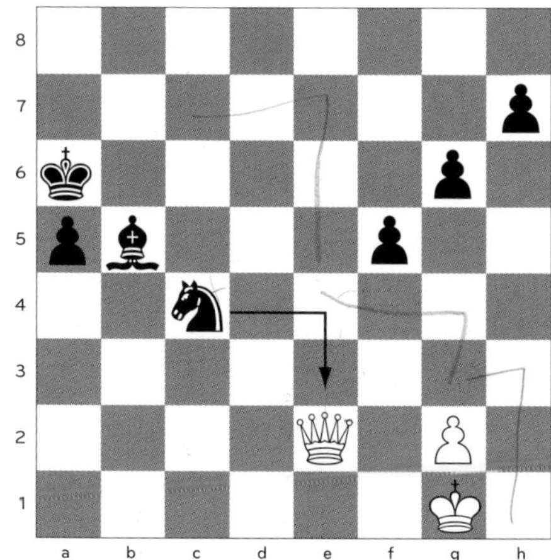

As you can see, all these sharp tactics are devastating. Look to use them on offense, and avoid them at all costs on defense!

RULE #3: LOOK BEFORE YOU LEAP

Remember this rule! It may seem easy to follow, but it has been the downfall of many good chess players in many important matches. Caution often separates good chess players from bad ones.

Before you make a move—and that means before you touch any of your pieces—you have to consider as many options as possible. Instead of marching blindly ahead, try out several possibilities in your mind. What will your opponent likely do if you make that move? Does the move improve your position? Does it strengthen you or weaken you? Does it accomplish anything? Will your opponent have a good countermove?

These are all important questions to ask yourself before each move. Then, when it's your opponent's move, instead of just sitting there watching him, try to focus on the bigger picture. Survey the entire battlefield: Where is your opponent trying to attack you? Where are you trying to mount your own attack? What are your weaknesses and strengths? Your opponent's?

Try to think as many moves ahead as possible. This is hard at first, but the better you get at thinking ahead, the better chess player you'll be—the same can be said about life in general!

CHAPTER THREE

THE OPENING

BY NOW, YOU ARE PROBABLY EAGER FOR BATTLE, and itching to play a real game of chess, if you haven't gone ahead and done it already! Well, General, since you're about to take personal command of your army and launch it into all-out war, the best advice we can give you is to concentrate first on the beginning of the game—the **opening**.

OPENING STRATEGIES

How does a great general get to be great? Why, by studying the tactics and strategies of great generals who have gone before him!

Chess has been around for thousands of years. So it's no wonder that, after all that time and all those trillions of chess games played, certain patterns of play have surfaced—especially at the start of games, when positions are simpler. These patterns, or series of moves, are called "chess openings." They have names and variations that have come down through the centuries, all saved for us by the miracle of chess notation.

There are limited possibilities for your first move, since all your pieces (except the knights) are stuck behind your pawns. Good moves at the start of a game are so limited that over centuries of chess playing, people have figured most of them out! These good moves tend to fall into certain patterns, or categories, and people have given names to these sequences of opening moves—colorful names like Giuoco Piano, Ruy Lopez, Queen's Gambit, and the Nimzo-Indian Defense.

Openings are often named for the pieces that are used, the places where they originated, or the people who developed them. Who knows—maybe someday you'll come up with an opening that will be named after you!

It's actually possible to learn some of these basic, tried-and-true sequences, and even memorize them if you want to go that far. The more familiar you are with openings, the better shape you'll be in when you reach the **middle game**, when most chess games are lost and won.

So pay close attention as we give you a crash course in how to start your battles on the chessboard.

Opening patterns are based on sound principles of chess strategy. Most

of these moves involve trying to develop your position quickly, control the center, and get the king into a protected spot, away from the action.

The following basic principles of the opening game will serve you well against any opponent. So don't feel like a copycat if you're playing a game of chess and your early moves follow a traditional opening. If you've studied the opening and know it well, you can be pretty sure you're on solid ground. The further into a traditional opening you get, though, the more variations there are, until pretty soon you're right in the thick of the middle game. From that point on, you're on your own.

DON'T TRY FOR A QUICK CHECKMATE

Fool's Mate aside—it's very difficult to checkmate your opponent during the opening of a game. There are just too many pawns and pieces in the way, and you don't have enough in position to attack. By going for a checkmate before your forces are ready, you may wind up in a weak position, or even lose material to your opponent! Before you can launch an attack, you must first advance your pieces, develop your position, and gain control of the center of the board.

CONTROLLING THE CENTER

The opening and middle parts of any chess game usually revolve around the **center** of the board. The squares e4, d4, e5, and d5 make up the center itself. Less vital but still important are the surrounding squares.

You can control the center directly by placing your own pawns and pieces there. Or you can do it from afar, by positioning your forces to attack anything that tries to move there. The player who controls these four squares and those surrounding them usually has the upper hand by the later stages of the game.

In your attempt to control the center, you'll want to advance your central pawns first, followed by your knights. Knights are usually the first pieces advanced during the opening because you don't have to move any pawns to free them from their opening

squares. One useful general rule about knights is try to keep them as close as possible to the center of the board, where they can move in all directions and control more squares. If a knight gets stuck in a corner, it can be hard (and will take a lot of time) to get it out! The spaces where they can best control the center are c3, f3, c6, and f6.

After your pawns and knights are in play, you'll want to develop your bishops, then safeguard your king (usually by castling), and only then bring your heavy pieces—queen and rooks—into the battle.

Controlling the center gives you enough room to maneuver into a good position to launch an attack. Behind your front lines, pieces can move closer to the action, or take control of open files and diagonals, or those that will soon open when your attack begins. By doing this, you will cramp your opponent's forces and she will find it difficult to move her pieces where she wants them to go; you will also isolate her key defenders away from the action. Also, if you succeed in taking over the middle of the board, it will be difficult if not impossible for your opponent to use her pieces to attack you!

DEVELOPING YOUR POSITION QUICKLY

In order to mount an attack on your opponent's king, you need a lot of power. Pawns alone won't do the trick, no matter how many of them you put in play. To be successful, you must free your important pieces to do what they do best!

As you can see from the board at the start of the game, each of your major pieces (except for your knights, which can jump over other pieces or pawns) is trapped behind a wall of pawns. That's why most openings feature pawns advancing to take control of the center of the board. But there's another reason to move your pawns forward—by doing so, you free up the more powerful weapons behind them!

A queen, a rook, or a bishop can move as many as seven spaces at a time in one direction. These pieces can control an entire file, rank, or diagonal, but only if nothing else is in the way. That's why it's important to line up your pawns properly in positions where they are protected and linked on touching files, but which also allow your pieces to get through. Whether you're planning an attack or building a solid defense, you need to look at how your pieces will be able to help. And the quicker you can get them into the thick of the battle, the better.

Later on in the game, when positions become locked and the board gets crowded, it can be more difficult to free up a piece and get it into the action. At that point, you may need to waste two or more moves to get the job done, handing the all-important initiative to your opponent. Early on, before the center gets too crowded, it's much easier. As we play through a few popular openings, watch to see how this is done.

PROTECTING YOUR KING

You'll notice that in many of the most popular openings, the two kings wind up castling early on. This is because castling is the best way to protect a king. Castling removes him from the central files where

the action is taking place. It keeps him off in a far corner, protected by a wall of pawns, and at the same time, frees a rook to get into the action as soon as possible. Of course, if you're castling, it means you've already launched your knight and bishop into the battle, since those pieces must be out of the way for you to do the move.

Notice also that queen-side castling is not used nearly as often as king-side castling. There are several reasons for this, but chief among them is that it takes longer to move three pieces—the knight, the bishop, *and* the queen—out of the way than two. King-side castling also puts your king closer to the corner and farther from the action than queen-side castling. Still, in certain circumstances, such as when your opponent is aiming an attack at the king side, you might want to remove your king to the opposite side of the board. That's when queen-side castling can really come in handy.

KEEPING YOUR QUEEN IN RESERVE

It is tempting to throw the queen's might into an early attack on your enemy, but beware! Don't bring your queen out to the center of the board right away. This makes your queen vulnerable to your opponent's attack, forcing repeated retreating or backward moves on your part and costing you the all-important initiative. While your queen is on the run, your opponent will be developing his pieces and taking over the center of the board. By moving the queen out too early, you may even expose her to the danger of capture. Losing your queen without capturing your opponent's queen, or at least a few lesser pieces, is a disaster for any chess player. In most cases, it's better to advance first with pawns and minor pieces. Bring the queen into the action only when you've prepared your ground and it's safe to do so.

GREAT OPENINGS

Except for very famous games that may acquire names of their own, such as Napoleon's Game with the Pope, chess games are named only by the two players involved and by the opening they chose to use. As we play through the following openings, you'll see the battle for the center take shape. You'll also understand why over hundreds of years many different ways of controlling the center have been developed.

KING'S PAWN OPENINGS

Most openings last seven to ten moves before shifting into middle game mode. Because controlling the center of the board is so important, most openings begin with White making one of two moves: e4, a king's pawn opening, or d4, a queen's pawn opening.

Let's look at a few, just to get a sense of why becoming familiar with common openings makes sense (it'll also give you a chance to practice reading chess notation). We'll tackle king's pawn openings first:

RUY LOPEZ

Ruy Lopez was a Spanish monk who lived back in the 1500s and loved to play chess. The opening he came up with back then is still one of the most popular today.

The Ruy Lopez is one of the oldest openings in existence and is typical of what is called an **open game**, meaning the game starts with both sides' king's pawns each advancing two spaces **1. e4... e5**. Open games tend to result in more wide-open middle game positions.

A **closed game** is one where White starts off playing **1. d4**, advancing his queen's pawn instead of his king's pawn. These games tend to progress into the pieces' having tightly packed positions that don't lend themselves to wide-open attacks.

Semi-open games begin as open games, with White playing **1. e4**, but instead of replying with **1. ...e5**, Black makes some other first move. These games tend to progress into the pieces' having unbalanced positions, with one player showing strength in one area and the other player having strength in another.

And now, the Ruy Lopez:

1. e4...e5
2. Nf3...Nc6

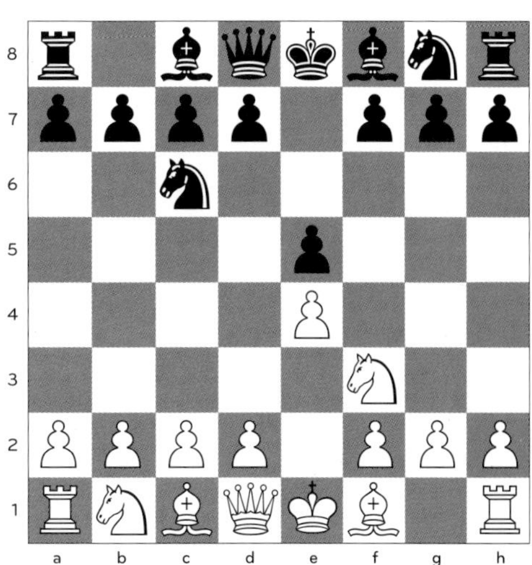

White's second move develops his knight, which now attacks Black's pawn, maintaining the initiative, as well as controlling the central square d4. Black responds with **2. ...Nc6**, protecting her pawn and challenging control of d4. There are several openings that begin with these same first two moves by both sides. White's third move, however, makes the opening a Ruy Lopez:

3. Bb5...

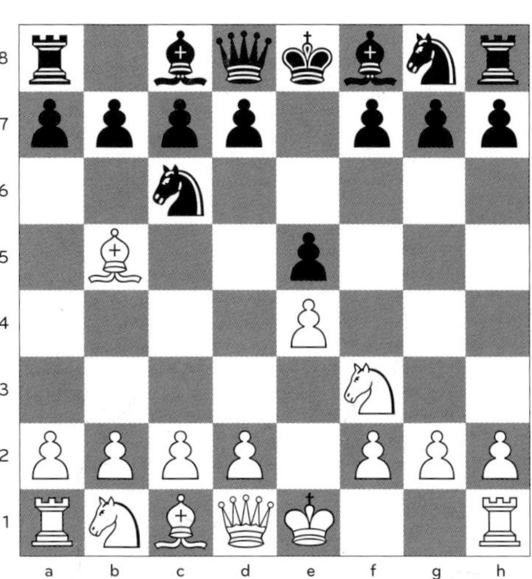

The bishop is now attacking Black's knight. If Black moves the knight, her pawn on e5 will be exposed to capture, with White taking a material advantage and controlling the central square e5. Luckily for Black, she doesn't *have* to move her knight because it's protected by two pawns. If the White bishop captures the Black knight, it will be captured in return, not a good exchange for White, because while two bishops can control the entire chessboard, one lone bishop can control only half the squares.

3. ...a6. (Ruy Lopez, Open Variation)

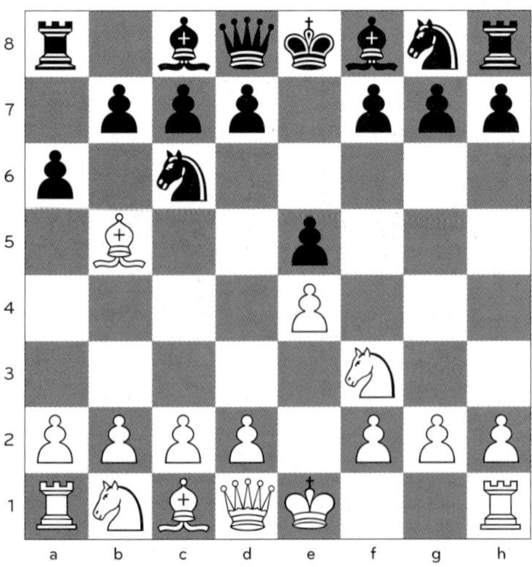

By advancing this pawn, Black is threatening the bishop, daring White to make the exchange of bishop for knight. If White accepts with **4. Bxc6**, Black can respond with **4. ...dxc6**. There follows **5. Nxe5...Qd4**, and after White either moves his threatened knight or protects it, Black gets the pawn back with **Qxe4** and develops it to a good position. Instead, White's best play is to refuse the exchange, moving the bishop to a safe square while still maintaining pressure on the Black knight, with **4. Ba4**. Black then plays **4. ...Nf6**. This develops her other knight and attacks White's king's pawn. **5. 0-0...** White castles, getting his rook into play. Now Black can respond in several ways. This is where "variations" of the Ruy Lopez happen.

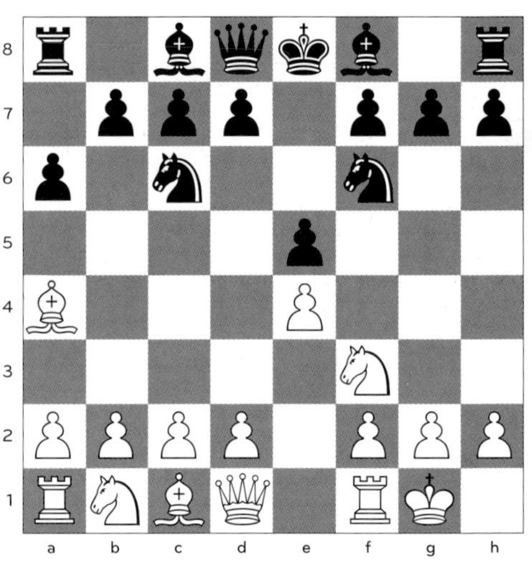

In the closed variation of this opening, Black plays **5. ...Be7**, getting ready to castle. This is followed by **6. Re1...b5**, **7. Bb3...d6**, and **8. c3...0-0**. The game is fairly even to this point. It is now time for White to build an attack before he loses the initiative.

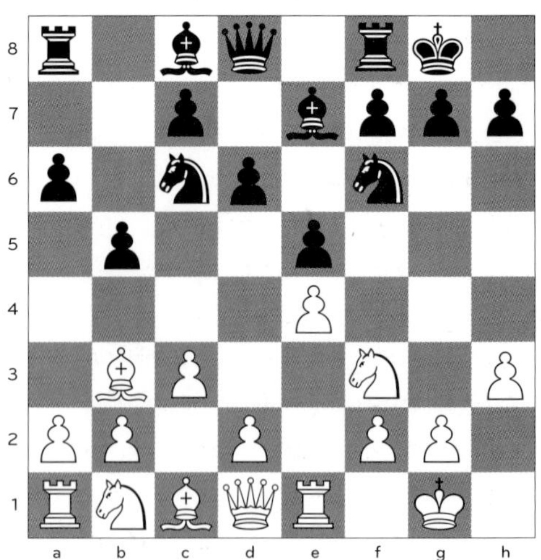

In the open variation, Black wastes no time getting at White with **5. ...Nxe4**. White responds with **6. d4...b5**, **7. Bb3...d5**, and **8. dxe...Be6**. This position gives White the possibility of building an attack on the king side, while Black has the advantage on the queen side.

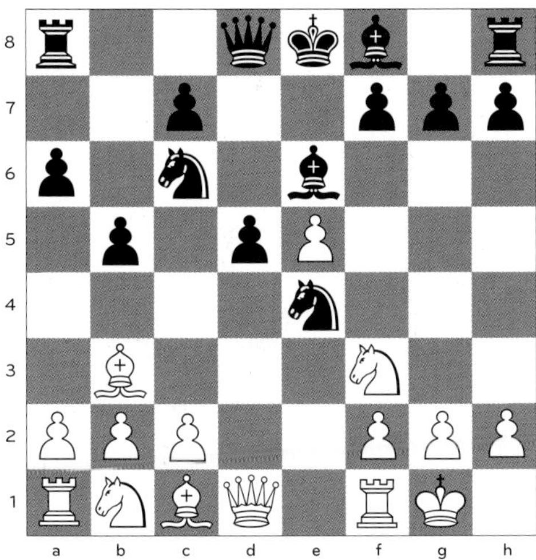

There are other variations as well, but the basic principles of Ruy Lopez are the same. The fight for the center is on from the very beginning, and both sides develop knights quickly and castle early.

The Ruy Lopez is a very successful opening for White. It has been calculated that White wins 56.5 percent of the time with this opener, a slightly higher percentage than usual. But that doesn't mean you shouldn't try it as Black—**1. ...e5** may suit your style, and you may get better results than the average player playing Black with this opening. All the openings we offer here—and most major openings—provide opportunities for both sides as the game goes on. These openings are used often, even by players at the highest level, and your choice of opening is basically a matter of style. With time, you'll sort out which openings you like best from either side of the board.

SICILIAN DEFENSE

The Sicilian Defense, named for the place where it originated, is one of the best openings for Black, which is why the word "defense" is in there. Black wins with this opening 48.5 percent of the time, about as good as it gets if you're playing the Black pieces. This opening is a semi-open game, where White starts by moving her king's pawn two spaces, but Black responds in a different way, throwing the game off-balance right at the start:

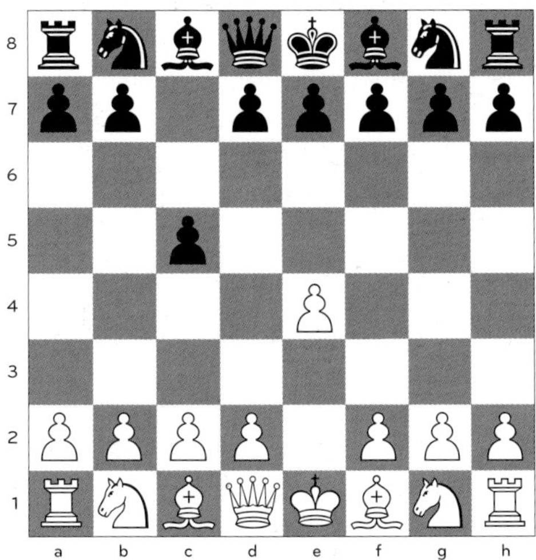

1. e4...c5.

Still, Black's move does put pressure on the central square d4.

2. Nf3...d6.

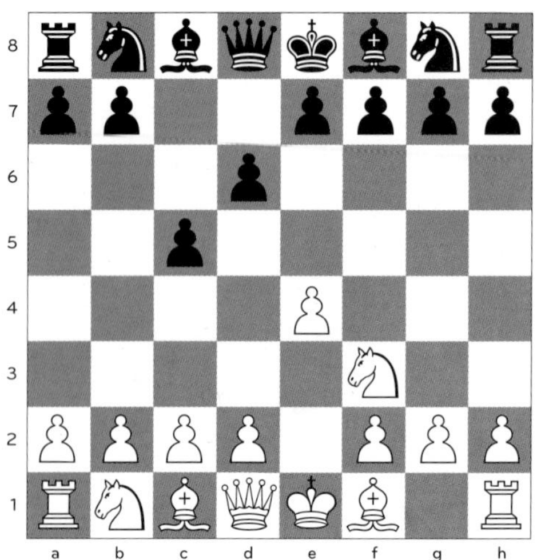

White develops his knight, and Black opens a diagonal for his bishop while preparing to challenge for the center later.

3. d4...cd (White offers an exchange of pawns, and Black accepts.)

4. Nxd4...Nf6

5. Nc3...

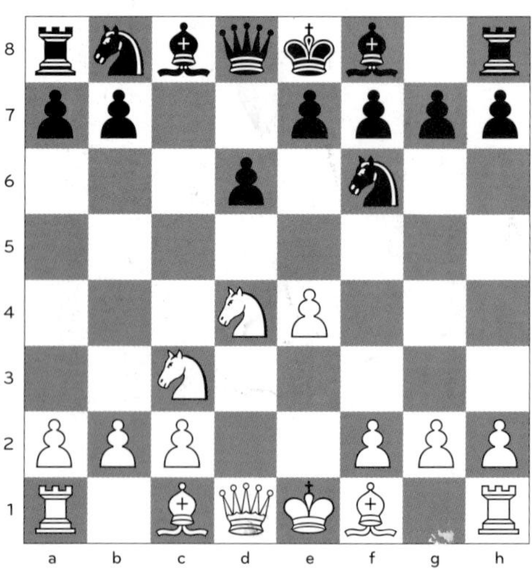

At this point, White's pieces are more developed than Black's (with two knights in play versus one), while Black has two central pawns, on the d and e files, to White's one at e4. Black can now play one of several moves, which begin different variations of the Sicilian Defense.

It's only natural that the more moves players make, the more variations there are to these standard openings. Think of an opening as a tree trunk and the variations are branches that sprout here and there. Those branches then sprout several other branches, and so on. In this book, to avoid confusion, we're sticking to the tree trunk and only one or two branches. As you develop your chess skills, you'll want to explore more and more variations of the popular openings to see which you like best.

In the Dragon Variation of the Sicilian Defense, Black responds with **5. ...g6,** preparing to get his king's bishop into the game. The variation follows with:

6. Be3...Bg7

7. f3...Nc6

8. Qd2...0-0

9. Bc4...Bd7

10. 0-0-0...Rc8.

As you can see, White controls more space. Now that she has castled queen side, she can begin to attack Black's king side by advancing her pawns and aiming her pieces at the defense in front of Black's king. But look at the c file—if Black moves his knight out of the way, his rook is in fine attacking position, with the White king in his sights behind all those blocking pieces or pawns. This will give Black the opportunity to seize the initiative should White make a mistake or falter in her attack.

QUEEN'S PAWN OPENINGS

The move **1. d4**, a queen's pawn opening, offers White many advantages. For one thing, the advanced pawn is protected by the queen. For another, it puts pressure on the c5 and e5 squares. If Black responds with e5, his pawn is lost.

QUEEN'S GAMBIT DECLINED

This opening is an example of a **closed game**, in other words, one that begins with White advancing his queen's pawn two spaces.

1. d4...d5

2. c4...

By making the move, White risks

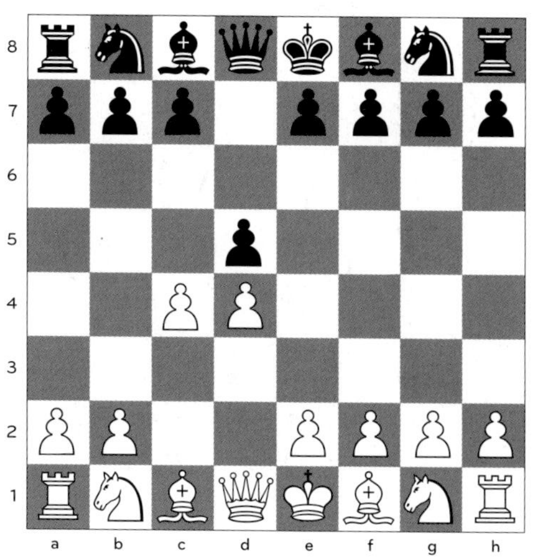

his pawn, but frees his pieces to operate. In fact, if the offered pawn is captured, it's White who gains by the sacrifice—which, when offered at the very start of the game, makes this type of opening a **gambit**—a situation in the opening where one player offers a material advantage to his opponent in exchange for positional advantage or the initiative.

See the gambit? White is offering to sacrifice his pawn. But if Black captures it with **2. ...dxc4** (Queen's Gambit Accepted, so called because White is offering a pawn on the queen's side of the board), White soon achieves a superior position with control of the center and better attacking possibilities. Most players decline the gambit because, after **2. ...dxc4**, **3. e4**, White controls all four center squares, and his bishop is now threatening to recapture the sacrificed pawn on c4.

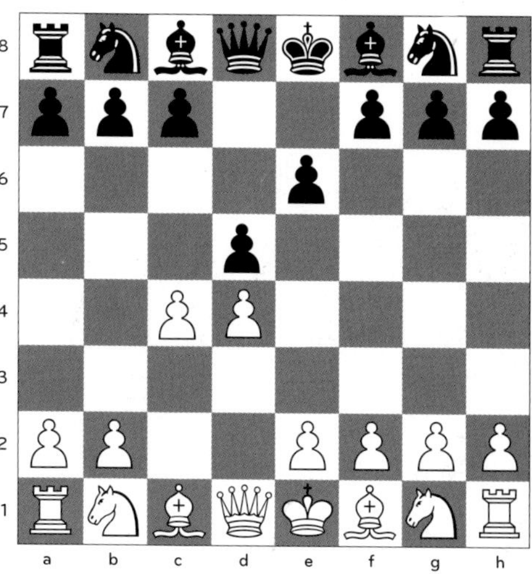

Black is well advised to decline, or refuse the gift, playing **2. ...e6** instead. This is the move that makes the opening a Queen's Gambit Declined. Typically, the opening would then proceed like this:

3. Nc3...Nf6

4. Bg5...Be7

5. e3...0-0

6. Nf3...Nbd7 (meaning the knight on the b file moves to d7, not the knight on the f file)

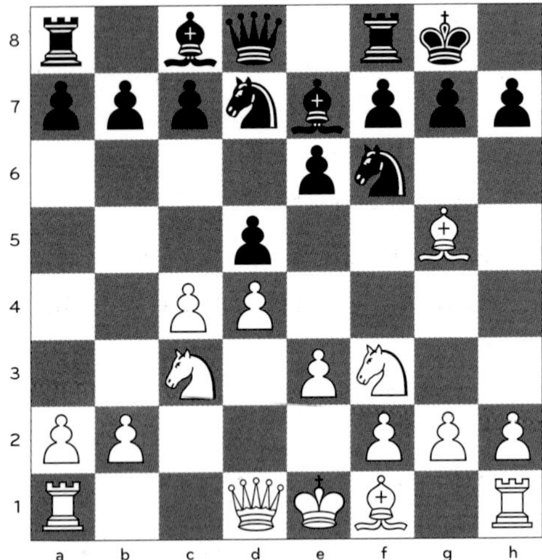

From this point on, there are too many variations to describe here. But whichever variation is followed, both sides have good possibilities for attack and counterplay (see page 62). Black will have to exchange a pawn for White's queen's pawn at some point in order to challenge him for control of the center. But at this point, it's still very much anybody's game.

KING'S INDIAN DEFENSE

This is a queen's pawn opening by White's choice, but it's called a "defense" because it is defined by how Black responds. It is Black, in this case, who dictates the direction of the game, even while White presses the initiative. Black's aim—a good one—is to quickly develop his pieces and get his king castled. He allows White to dominate the center temporarily, figuring that he will be able to challenge it later, when White has to pause to patch up weaknesses in her position.

1. d4...Nf6

2. c4...g6

3. Nc3...Bg7

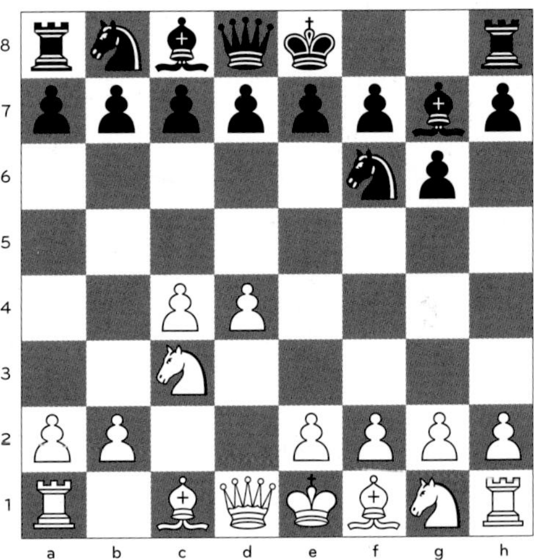

Black's first three moves have all served to put his bishop in position to attack the center from afar. As we mentioned before, this is called a **fianchetto**. You move your bishop into the battle by placing it in the second rank in front of the knight's starting spot. To do this, you need to move the knight's pawn forward one square. Meanwhile, Black has already cleared his king for castling!

4. e4...d6

This last move of Black's keeps White from advancing her king's pawn to e5 and threatening Black's knight. In the Samisch Variation, White now moves **5. f3**. In the Classical Variation, she moves her knight instead. Either way, Black's next move is to castle.

5. Nf3...0-0

6. Be2...e5

7. 0-0...Nc6

8. d5...Ne7

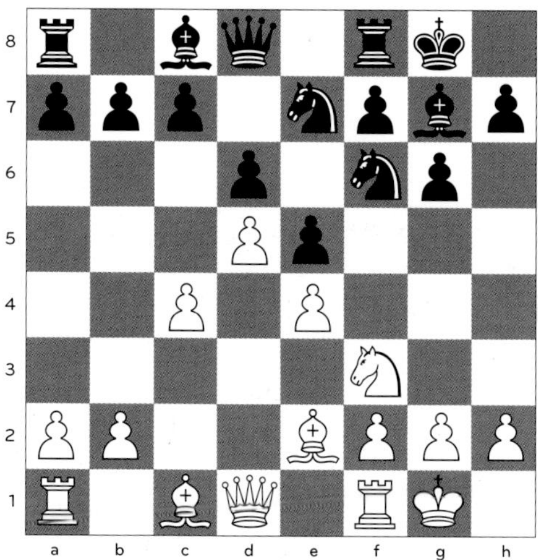

The Classical Variation leaves both sides with a locked, or "closed," position in the center. Black has better attacking chances on the king side, but this is counterbalanced by White's superior development on the queen side. It's a pretty even game at this point.

The King's Indian Defense is a "modern" chess opening. In the old days, those playing Black would always try and challenge directly for control of the center by placing pawns there. In the early twentieth century, however, the famous chess master Aron Nimzowitsch came up with the radical idea that, as Black, you can challenge for control of the center from afar, and commit your pawns later. The Nimzo-Indian Defense, a variant of the King's Indian, is named after him.

FLANK OPENINGS

Although most openings start with a pawn advance aimed at controlling the center of the board, there are a few openings that don't start that way, but still turn out pretty well for the player who employs them. These are called **flank openings** because they direct force from the flanks, or sides, of the board toward the center, instead of immediately attempting to control the center with pawns. Here's one such opening that shows off some of the more modern theories of chess strategy:

ENGLISH OPENING

This opening was named for the Englishman Howard Staunton, who first made it popular:

1. c4

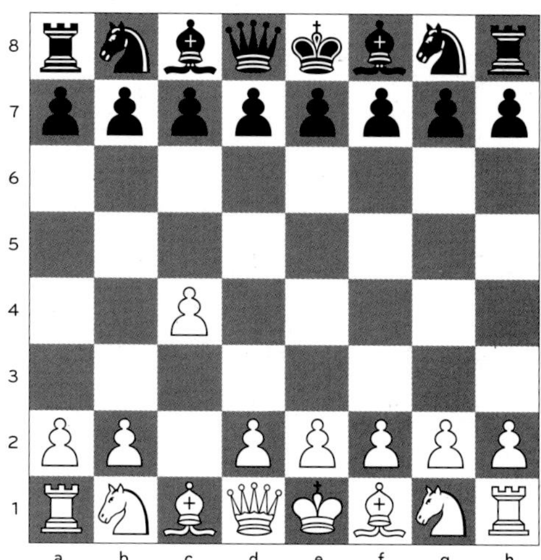

This unconventional first move is designed to control the center from the flank, or side, instead of directly, with either d4 or e4. This is one of the reasons why it's called a flank opening.

1. ...e5
2. Nc3...Nf6
3. Nf3...Nc6

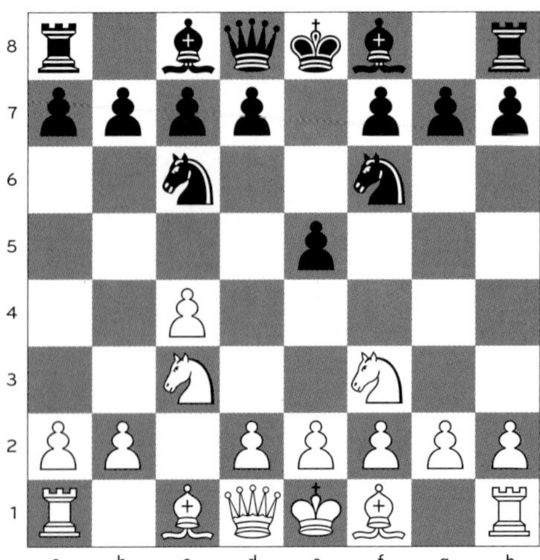

White is trying to control the center—particularly the d5 square—while Black has replied more traditionally, occupying the e5 square. Both sides have quickly moved their knights into the action.

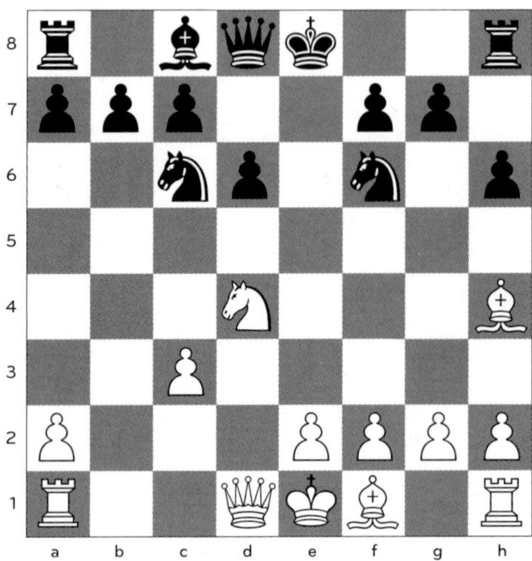

4. d4...exd
5. Nxd4...Bb4
6 Bg5...h6
7. Bh4...Bxc3
8. bxc...d6.

At this point, each side has its strengths and weaknesses. White has two bishops, while Black has only one. White also has a bigger presence in the center. But Black has created a weakness on White's queen side, where White's pawns will be hard to defend (see "Pawn No-No's," page 65). This is not your usual opening by any means! Neither side is particularly well developed yet, and there are imbalances all over the board. It's going to be a bumpy ride the rest of this game!

There are many more chess openings to explore—hundreds, if you count all the popular variations. You might want at some point to learn a few of them by heart. If so, you can find books in the chess section of any bookstore, or on the Internet, which have dozens of annotated openings for you to learn. But for now, it's enough if you understand the basic principles that make for some good opening moves.

CHESS PROBLEMS FROM THE OPENING

You can find the answers on page 113.

PROBLEM 1

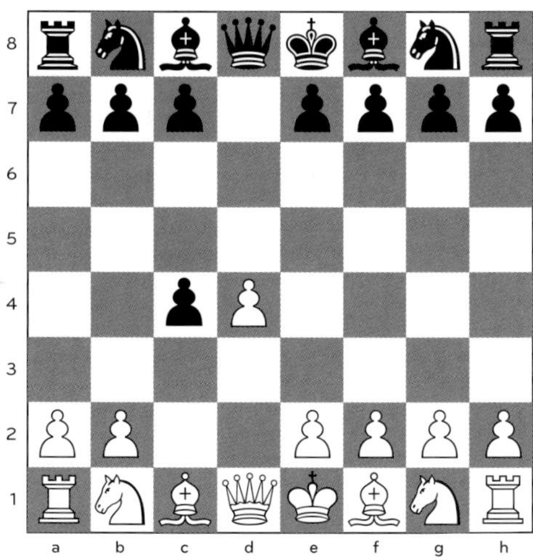

If Black accepts the gambit pawn by playing **2. ...dxc4**, what is a good move which takes advantage of Black losing control over the e4 square?

PROBLEM 2

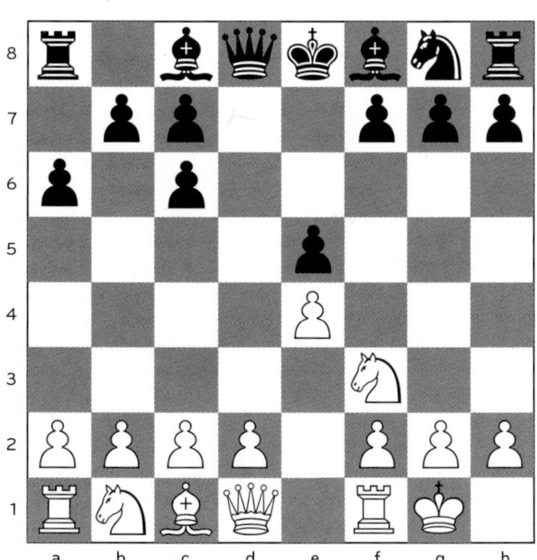

In the exchange variation of the Ruy Lopez, White can play **5. 0-0**. What should Black do next?

PROBLEM 3

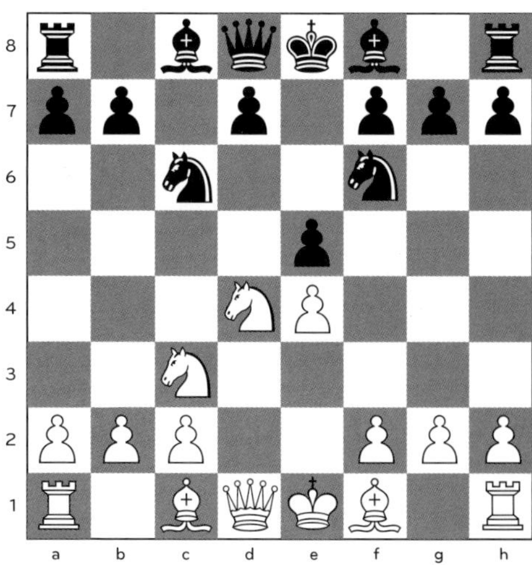

Here, Black has chosen the Sveshnikov (also known as the Pelikan) variation of the Sicilian Defense. Black attacks White's knight and drives it from the center of the board. The cost for doing so is that the d5 square will now be a permanent weakness and black's d-pawn is now a backward pawn (as discussed on page 66). Where should White's knight go to?

PROBLEM 4

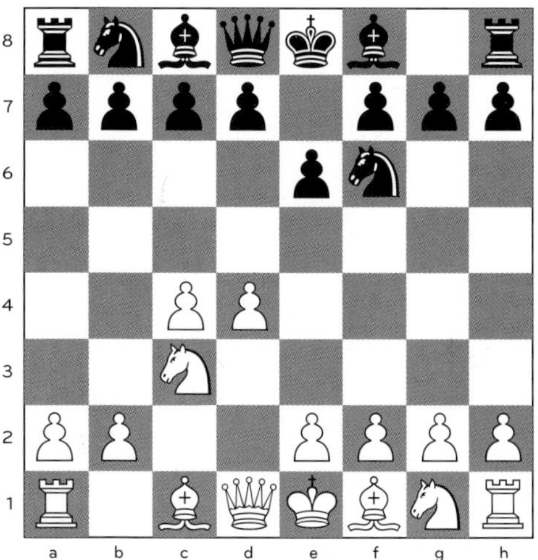

White has just played **3. Nc3**. What does White wish to play next? What is Black's best way to prevent this?

CHAPTER FOUR

THE MIDDLE GAME

WELL, GENERAL, NOW YOU'VE HAD YOUR FIRST taste of combat. You've learned about the opening maneuvers, and the basic strategies needed to put yourself in good, solid shape for the middle game.

As you survery your forces at the end of the opening, you can see that the board now looks different than it did at the start. Pieces and pawns are threatening each other. Kings are perhaps castled. Weaknesses have begun to emerge. It's time to exert some brute force and take control of the battle!

PRINCIPLES OF THE MIDDLE GAME

It's our hope that you've arrived at this point with your king out of danger, and your central pawns advanced and supported by your minor pieces, which you've moved into position to control the center. Now, you need to make a plan of attack, and muster the forces to carry it out. Don't forget, though, that your opponent is doing the very same thing! It's important not to forget your defense while getting ready to attack.

Of course, two opposing armies can't just develop their positions on the board without eventually running into each other and doing battle. Before we sound the trumpets and the fight begins in earnest, let's go over a few basic principles of the middle game:

MOBILITY

Having **mobility** and being able to maneuver your pieces is the key to a successful attack. It doesn't hurt your defense either. During the middle game, try to get as many of your pieces involved in the game as possible. But remember, getting and keeping the initiative is also important. Don't waste moves bringing more pieces into the battle unless you're sure you can spare that time!

BUILDING STRENGTH AND CREATING WEAKNESS

At this point, either you or your opponent, or both, will have one or more weaknesses in their positions. Try to spot them—both yours and the enemy's. Are there any poorly defended squares that you can put pressure on, expanding your zone of control? Can you line up more than one piece in position to launch an attack? Do you have any weaknesses of your own that you need to tighten up before trying to attack your opponent?

ATTACK AND COUNTERPLAY

Gaining the initiative is important, but you can only hold it for so long without launching an attack, because the other player will be plotting mischief against you the whole time, looking for her own chance to strike! Remember, once you start an attack, you've got to be able to sustain it, or your opponent can quickly begin one of her own!

Rule #2, if you recall, is that the best defense is a good offense—in chess, that's called "counterplay." For instance, if one player is trying an attack on the king side of the board, the other player, instead of just playing defense, may be able to stop her opponent's attack by launching her own attack on the queen side! Of course, if your pieces are mobile and have room to maneuver, you should be able to respond to any counterattack.

TO TRADE OR NOT TO TRADE?

Sooner or later, in any chess game, pieces and pawns get captured.

Sometimes this happens because one player has forgotten to protect that piece or pawn or move it out of harm's way. If you can capture an enemy piece or pawn without giving up any material of your own, that piece or pawn is said to be *en prise* (French for "seized," or literally "in grip"). But more often, a piece or

pawn is either captured as a sacrifice or as part of an exchange or trade.

Players choose to exchange pieces and pawns for a variety of reasons. You might see an opportunity to get a material advantage by taking more value points from your opponent's army than you give up from your own. Or you might want to open up a file, diagonal, or rank for one of your pieces to move through. You might want to discover or create a flaw in your enemy's position or get rid of one in your own. Whatever the reason, it's important to try to get some advantage, whether it's material or position, from every exchange. The only case where you'd want to lose pawns or pieces on purpose is if it lets you win bigger eventually (see "The Art of Sacrifice," page 72).

Most of the time, **winning an exchange** is a good thing. It means you have more pieces and pawns, or at least, more "power points," than your opponent. As we said before, any material advantage, even having one extra pawn, can win you a game of chess. So by all means, try to make sure you win material in any exchange—or at least come out even—and that you don't lose any pieces or pawns needlessly.

When you are ahead in material, trading pieces and pawns generally benefits you. Your opponent's troops will get smaller, and your extra units will be able to win the game more easily since there won't be much left to oppose them. For instance, having an extra pawn may not seem like much of an advantage in the middle game, but in the endgame, the board will be more open, and that extra pawn may be able to make it all the way to the back row—and a promotion! On the other hand, if you're down in material, try to avoid letting go of any more of it, unless it gives you some other advantage.

But remember, capturing a piece requires spending one move. That move may leave you out of position, or vulnerable to attack, forcing you to move the same piece again, or spend a move getting another piece out of harm's way. That delay in your game plan may be enough to let your opponent seize the initiative—it could even cost you the game!

MIDDLE GAME STRATEGIES

PAWNS

The best chess master of the eighteenth century, François-André Danican Philidor, once said that "pawns are the soul of chess." What he meant was that where the pawns are placed is a more important factor in the game than where the pieces are placed.

During the opening, you've tried to advance your pawns to control the center of the board. You've gotten them out of the way of your pieces so that your knights and bishops are now in play. It is our hope that your pawns are in good positions and are aligned.

What does this mean to have your pawns aligned? Well, let's start with the fact that pawns aren't very powerful alone. They can only move forward (except when they capture), and except for their first moves, they can only move one square at a time. They are easily blocked, either by other pawns or pieces—sometimes even your own! Pawns are more powerful when used together, and the best position for them to be arranged is in linked diagonal or zigzag chains so that one pawn protects the other. This is how you align your pawns into a **pawn chain**.

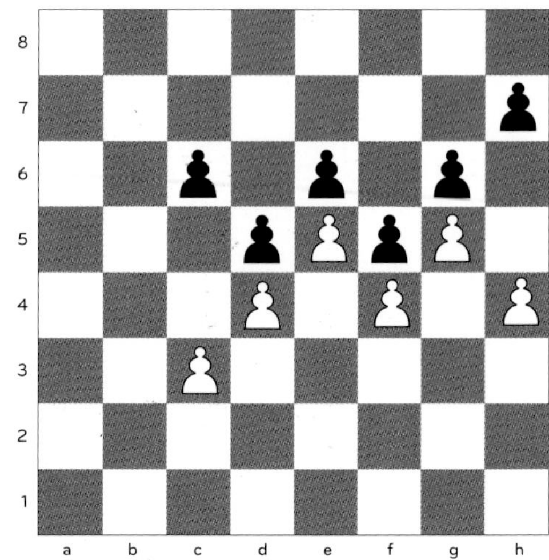

Look at this diagram. White's pawns are linked in a protective chain that controls the central squares (c3, d4, e5, f4, g5, h4). Black's pawns are also linked (c6, d5, e6,f5, g6, h7), but because White has advanced into Black's territory, Black's position is somewhat more cramped and he will have some difficulty moving his pieces. White has more mobility, and therefore, better attacking chances.

Keep in mind that, even with a strong pawn chain, there are always places to attack a piece. The rearmost pawn in a chain is always the most vulnerable because none of the other pawns can protect it. So if you're the opposing player, look to take advantage of that weakness! Think of a pawn chain as a tree—if you want to chop it down, you start hacking at the bottom. Once you capture the rearmost pawn in the chain, the one just in front of it can then be easily captured too.

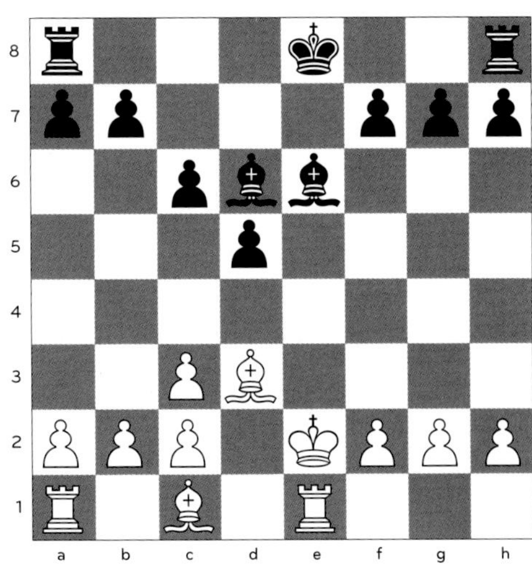

PASSED PAWNS

Passed pawns are pawns that have advanced far enough so that they cannot any longer be captured by enemy pawns on either side of them.

Once a pawn becomes a passed pawn, it becomes a grave danger to the other side, because it now takes pieces, not pawns, to stop it from reaching the back rank and being promoted. So by all means, try to turn your pawns into passed pawns during the middle game—but be sure your passed pawns are connected to a pawn chain. If a passed pawn is too far out in front of your other pawns, it can easily be isolated and captured. Moving a pawn too far, too fast is a pawn no-no! Speaking of which . . .

PAWN NO-NO'S

DOUBLED PAWNS

Doubled pawns—two pawns on the same file—are usually weak because they're not in position to protect one another. In fact, they're sort of like having two left feet! In the diagram, White has two pawns on the c file. One of those pawns got there from the d file, so there is no pawn left on that file.

When pawns are next to each other, they can protect each other. As one advances, the other is diagonally behind it, ready to capture any enemy that attacks the forward pawn. It's just like two feet walking up the chessboard. But when pawns are doubled, one gets in the way of the other. They can't protect each other. Doubled pawns can easily become isolated from all your other pawns, since they're already deprived of protection on one side.

ISOLATED PAWNS

Look at Black's king's pawn all alone in its position. There is no pawn on either side of it to protect it—it's an **isolated pawn**.

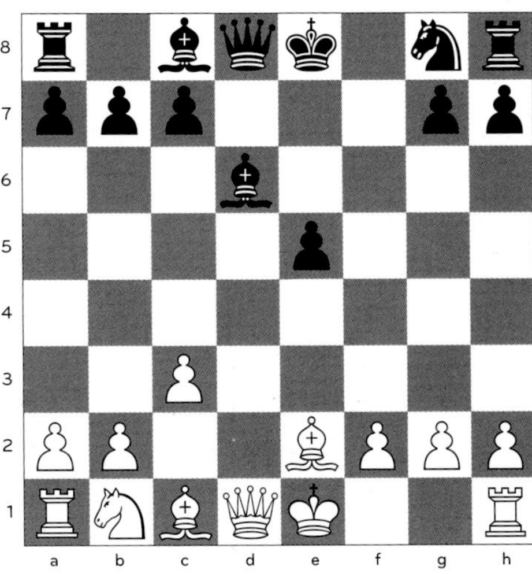

Black will have to use a piece instead of a pawn to protect this vulnerable pawn. If this isolated pawn is blocked by one of White's pieces, no Black pawn can be advanced to threaten the blocking piece. Don't leave a pawn alone!

OVEREXTENDED AND BACKWARD PAWNS

When you advance one pawn so far ahead of the others that it's left exposed, it's called an *overextended pawn* because it's hard to protect and easily captured. A *backward pawn*, on the other hand, is one that's left behind, so that there are no other pawns to protect it now or in the future. These are both weak positions to be in. Keep your pawns linked whenever possible so that they can protect each other and block enemy advances!

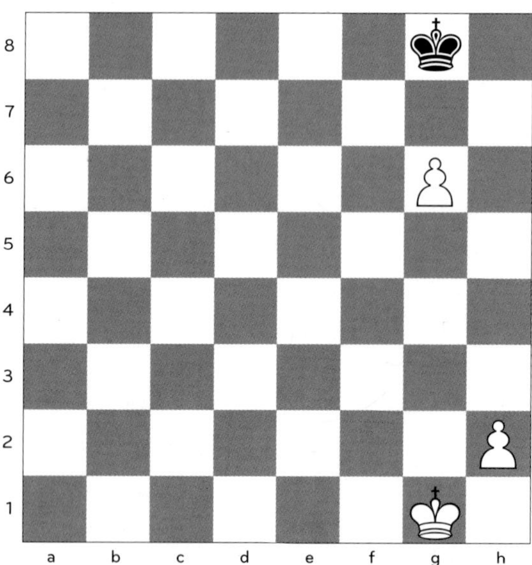

White has foolishly moved his king's knight pawn all the way to the sixth rank, while his other pawn is still back on the second rank. The overextended pawn at g6 can be easily captured by Black's king in two moves, while it will take the White king four moves to protect it.

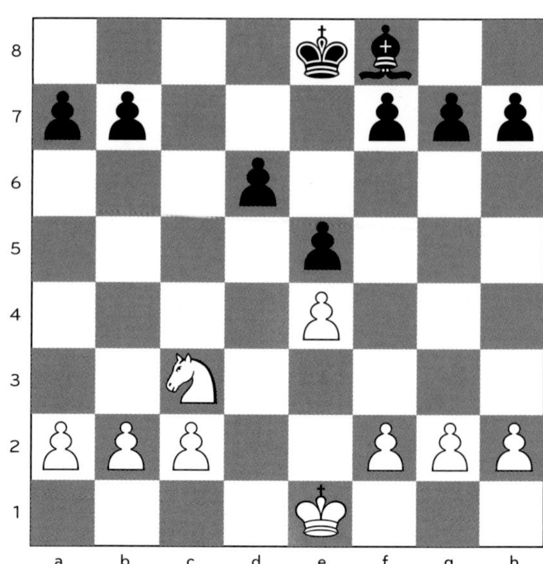

Here, Black's queen pawn is behind her king pawn. There is no queen bishop pawn. Therefore, the queen pawn will never be able to move ahead without being captured. This backward pawn will never have another pawn which can defend it, and will be much easier for White to capture.

Advancing your pawns is good as long as you have a good reason to do so. Never advance a pawn just because you can't think of anything better to do with your move. Think harder instead! Once you advance a pawn, you can't move it back—you're committed to defending it. Remember, pawns, unlike pieces, can't move backward, sideways, or any other way but forward.

PAWN GRABBING

Sometimes it's tempting to take every enemy piece or pawn you can. It's good to get ahead in material, but beware of poisoned gifts! Sometimes, spending the time to take a pawn—which, after all, is worth only one value point—costs you a critical tempo or winds up opening the door for an enemy attack! Capturing a pawn may also take one of your key pieces out of the action or remove it from a strong square to a weaker one.

Let's say your opponent has one or more weakened pawns. Should you devote your attentions to capturing them, thereby getting yourself ahead in material? Consider carefully: Material advantage is good, but not if it comes at the cost of the initiative or position, such as control of the center, or an open file, rank, or diagonal. And especially not if by grabbing that pawn, you're ignoring an attack by your opponent! Always remember the three factors to consider in judging any position: material, position, and initiative!

ROOKS

By the middle game, your minor pieces—your bishops and knights—should be out and in the thick of the battle. Your rooks, however, may still be in the corners on the back rank—now's the time to get them into the action. In addition to castling, rooks are great for launching attacks since they have a wide range of movement.

Rooks are mighty warriors, but they also have a weakness. Rooks begin the game in the corner of the board, trapped and far from the action, on squares a1, a8, h1, and h8. The player who succeeds in freeing his rooks and using them in battle before his opponent does is usually going to come out on top. As with the queen, you don't want to bring them out before your pawns and minor pieces are competing for the center and your king is secured. But once you've accomplished those opening goals, don't forget to bring your rooks into the battle!

As we've already mentioned, try to use your rooks to control open files—those with no pawn or only a weak pawn on them—by lining them up on the home rank of those files.

The best of all rook moves is to eventually get one or both rooks to the seventh rank for White, second rank for Black. This is sometimes called "getting a pig" because of all the pieces and pawns you can greedily gobble up in this mighty position. Unless your opponent can quickly come up with some counterplay, your "pig" is likely to prove fatal to his game.

BISHOPS

Bishops in the middle game are very useful in attacking the king down the long diagonals. Often a bishop may pair up with a queen to threaten checkmate. Keeping the bishop in a corner where it can command that long diagonal may be a good idea, but only if the board remains open enough for the bishop to command all those squares. In the middle game, it's not uncommon for bishops of either color to find themselves isolated from the action, blocked by a wall of pawns.

This is good, as long as it's not one of *your* bishops.

If you have only one bishop, it's generally best to align your pawns on the opposite square color. Otherwise, your bishop won't be able to move around very well. On the other hand, if *your opponent* only has a bishop that moves on, say, the light squares, you'll want to align your pawns on light squares, too, so he can't get past them to attack your king. But try to keep both your bishops—as you can see, they are especially powerful when used in pairs to cover the whole board.

Note that having both a pair of bishops and a pair of knights working together is desirable. Having one bishop and one knight makes it more difficult for a player to make them work together, since you lose the ability of twin bishops to cover all squares on the board and the ability of both knights to protect each other at the same time. Making a bishop and a knight work together can be done, but it takes a lot of skill and practice.

QUEEN

At the center of most attacks in the middle game is the powerful queen. We hope you've kept her safe till now, first advancing your pawns and developing your minor pieces to control the center of the board. Now you can bring in the mighty queen.

Try to identify squares to apply pressure to with your queen—does your opponent have a weak pawn, or a piece that can be trapped and captured? Try to attack these weak pieces and pawns by threatening them with mounting pressure using another piece along with the queen. If your opponent's piece or pawn is protected by one other piece, attack it with two. If it's protected by two pieces, attack with three! Use your queen to keep your other pieces protected from afar. Use her to back up a rook on an open file or a bishop on an open diagonal. Or use her to keep the enemy's king in check or his pieces on the run. If you use your queen together with all your other soldiers, you will be unstoppable! In fact, along with back-rank checkmates (see page 70), "queen and helper" checkmates, where the attacking queen is protected by another piece or pawn, are the most common in chess.

KING

Once you've castled, your king is out of the way until the endgame, protected by a wall of pawns and perhaps a knight, but he's not yet completely safe. If your opponent should attack, with one of her pieces reaching your home rank, your king could be trapped behind his own pawns and checkmated by an enemy rook or queen! This is called a **back-rank checkmate**.

At some point before that happens, you need to find time to provide your king with an escape square, or luft. This means advancing a pawn to create an empty, protected square on the second rank (or the seventh if you're Black) where your king can move to escape danger. Most times, you'll want to move your pawn to h3 (or h6 for Black).

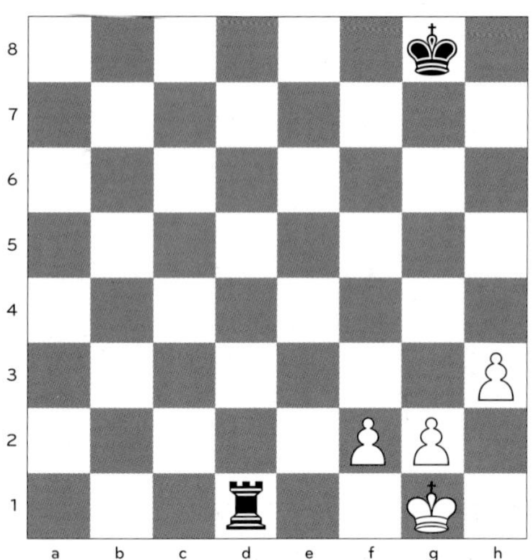

Sometimes you might want to move the g pawn forward one square, as part of a fianchetto maneuver, or even move your f pawn. But beware—all these moves, especially the last, can backfire later because they weaken the protective wall around your king.

The f pawn is especially weak. When moved before castling, it opens you to an early defeat (as we saw in Fool's Mate). It is also vulnerable to attack when left in place, unless it is well protected (as we saw in Scholar's Mate). In fact, most early mates occur against the f pawn.

Even after castling, moving the f pawn opens the king to attack from the center and opposite sides of the board, while moving the h pawn to create luft only risks attack from the h2 or h7 square.

To sum up: Don't make those moves in front of a castled king until you have to, but don't forget to make them before trouble arrives at your back door!

KNIGHTS

Knights are usually the first pieces advanced during the opening because you don't have to move any pawns to free them from their opening squares. As we mentioned before, try to keep your knights as close as possible to the center of the board, where they can move freely and show off their strength.

During the middle game, knights are great for controlling the center and defending the king while the other pieces—those with a longer range like bishops and queens—go on the attack. But the knight's ability to leap over other pieces and pawns gives it a real advantage in closed, blocked-off positions. In a game where not a lot of pieces or pawns have been captured, knights may be the only pieces able to get through a crowded board for an attack on enemy pieces!

A pair of knights is a good thing to have in the middle game, since they can

be positioned to protect one another and still command a wide range of squares. For instance, if one knight is on the back rank in order to block an enemy pawn from converting, the other can be in position to protect it, and vice versa. In the same way, a knight controlling a central square and the other knight off to the side can protect one another, making it hard to capture them.

In general, during the middle game, you want to advance your knights in the direction of the enemy king. They should always be on the lookout for weakened pawns, unprotected pieces, and forking opportunities. Knights are the best pieces for pulling surprise attacks, since it's hard to visualize where they might go next!

THE ART OF SACRIFICE

Sometimes you give up pieces on purpose. This is called a **sacrifice** (if it happens in the opening, it's called a gambit—see the section entitled "Queen's Gambit Declined," page 55). You may sacrifice material to gain an advantage in position or initiative (time). You might give up material to open a file or diagonal for attack. Or you might employ a **decoy sacrifice**, designed to lure your opponent's piece away from the action, where it will be less useful to him in defense.

For beginners, sacrificing is probably not a very good idea. It takes practice and experience to win when you're at a material disadvantage. But it's an exciting chess game when a player wins after sacrificing a piece. Even though it's not advised for a beginner to sacrifice his pieces, read the following game example to gain inspiration. Maybe one day soon you, too, will be sacrificing pieces for the greater good of your game.

The sample game that follows features the great American nineteenth-century grandmaster Paul Morphy against an amateur player. Unfair, you say? Maybe—but it sure makes for an interesting study. Besides, to make it a fair fight with an amateur opponent, Morphy played the game with a handicap—no queen's rook! See if you can use your knowledge of chess notation to follow and understand this exciting game.

PAUL MORPHY (WHITE) VS. AMATEUR OPPONENT (BLACK)

GIUOCO PIANO OPENING

The Giuoco Piano (Italian for "Quiet Joke") is an old opening that isn't used much these days. It originated in the seventeenth century and was also called "the Italian Game" after a famous Italian chess player, Gioachino Greco, who often used the opening. Giuoco Piano tends to result in even positions on both sides, and a lot of drawn games. Not in this case, though!

1. e4...e5
2. Nf3...Nc6

Recognize the opening? It's the same as Ruy Lopez. But now it takes a different turn:

3. Bc4...Bc5

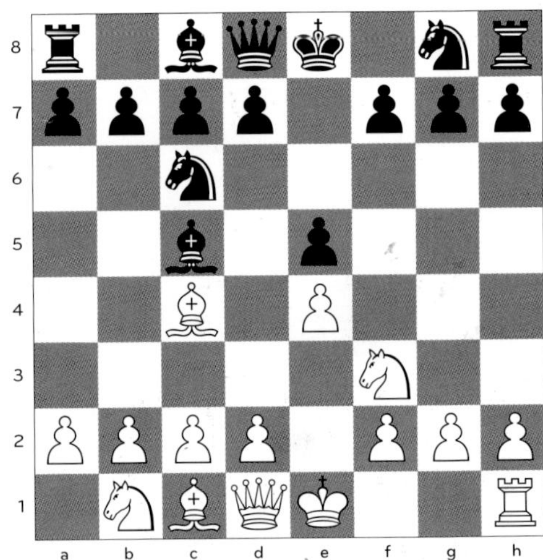

This is the Giuoco Piano Opening. Morphy continues with a common variation known as the Evans Gambit:

4. b4...Bxb4
5. c3...Bc5

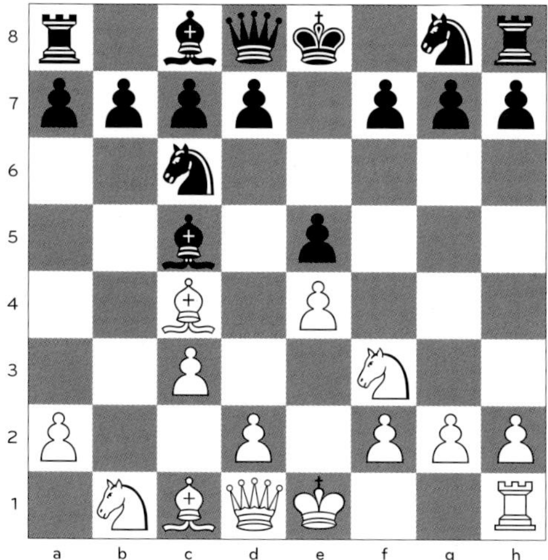

Notice that while Black gains a pawn here, he has also spent two moves placing his bishop right back where it was before. Morphy gains two tempi, the plural of tempo, and uses it to open up the board and take the lead in development. So, remember, if you're ahead in development, try to open the board up, and if you're behind, try to keep the position as closed and locked up as possible!

6. d4...exd

7. 0-0

Has Morphy goofed? Already down a rook to begin the game, and having given up his queen's knight's pawn in favor of

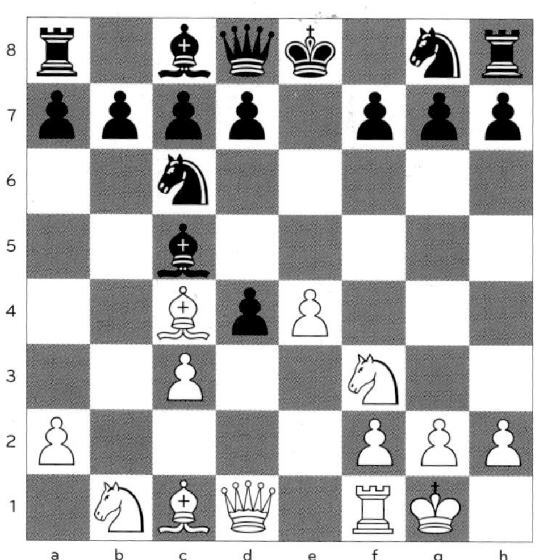

rapid development, doesn't he need to recapture the pawn he's lost at once with **7. cd**? Besides, if he doesn't take the Black pawn, what stops Black from grabbing yet another pawn with **7. ...dc**?

Well, as it turns out, this is the heart of the Evans Gambit. Morphy can afford to take the time out to castle. If Black does grab his pawn, he can respond with **8. Nxc3**. This gives him an overwhelming lead in development and lots of attacking possibilities—he controls the open d file, the c1 to g6 diagonal, and the open e file if he moves his rook to e1. So Black retreats with:

7. ...Bb6

8. cxd...d6

9. Nc3...

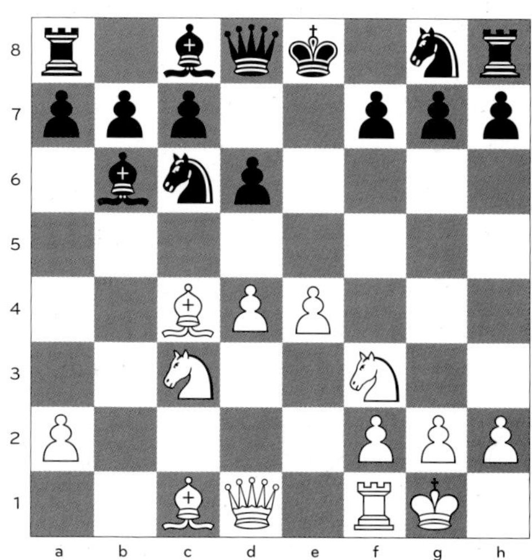

This is the typical Evans Gambit. White has the better position, and Black, with the material advantage, decides to go on the attack before it's too late.

9 ...Na5

10. Bd3...Bg4 (a little too aggressive, considering Black's poor development. He's better off here with **10. ...Nge7**.)

11. Be3...Qf6

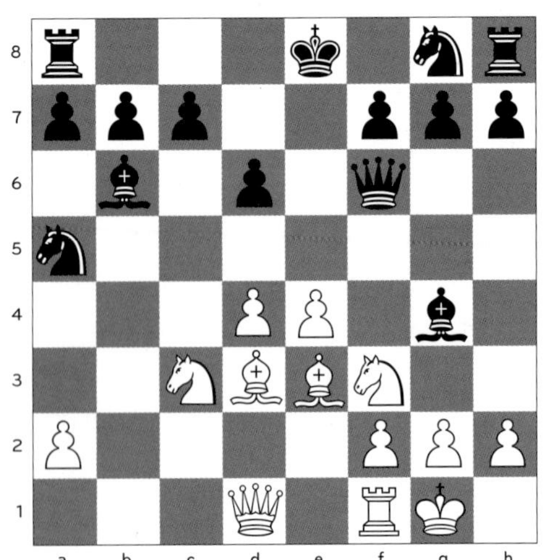

Black moves his queen into the action way too early. Remember, we warned you about that earlier? Morphy will now make him pay.

12. Nd5...Qd8 (a waste of two moves for Black, while Morphy just keeps on advancing)

13. h3...Bxf3 (trading down, as players with a material edge are supposed to do)

14. Qxf3...Nf6

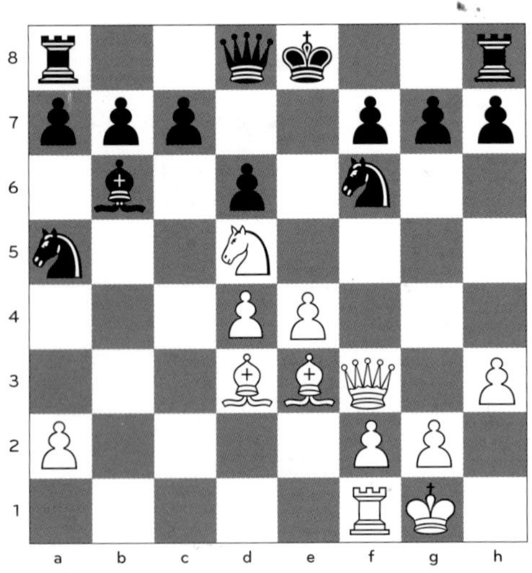

Black is starting to develop now, but it's way too late. Morphy is ready to move in for the kill:

15. Bg5...Bxd4

16. e5...Bxe5 (Morphy's sacrificing material left and right, but he knows what he's doing!)

17. Re1!!...0-0

18. Rxe5...dxe5

19. Nxf6+...gxf6

20. Bxf6!!

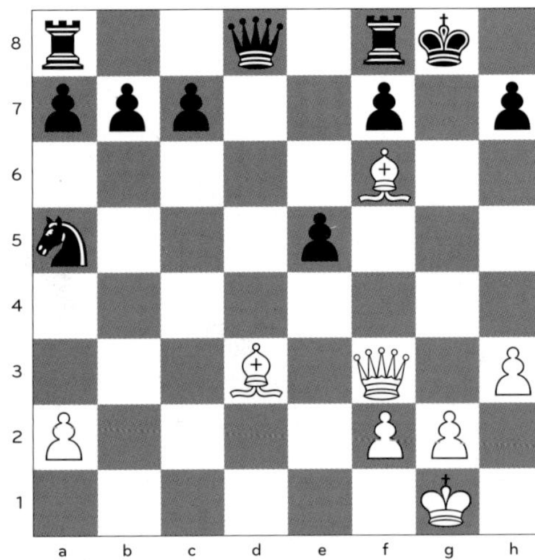

Black is about to lose his queen. He has to use it to take the White bishop on f6, or White will play **21. Qg3#**! Morphy wins this game in spite of giving up so much material because he succeeds in opening lines for his rooks, bishops, and queen.

KING-SIDE ATTACKS

As we've pointed out before, one of your main objectives during the opening is to get your king safely castled. That's because your opponent's main goal is to go after him with a king-side attack. Sure, your opponent can do a queen-side attack too—but usually that's because your king side has a strong defense, or because he wants to draw your attention away from his own king-side attack and trick you on the queen side of the board.

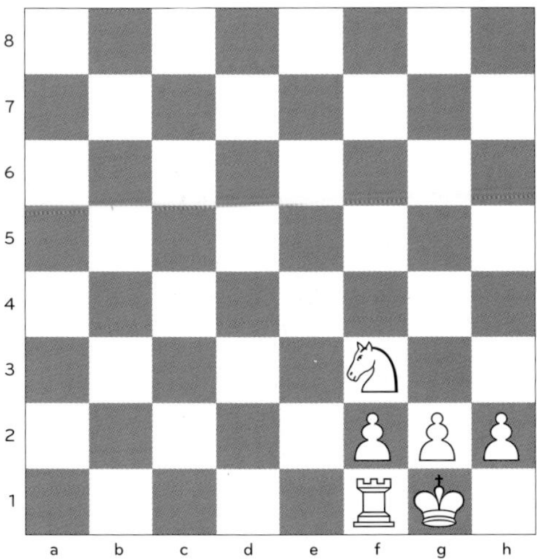

This diagram shows the ideal king-sided castling position. Notice that the pawns form a tight, protective row. The rook blocks access along the home rank, and the knight is itself protected by the pawn on g2. There is no way, in this position, for the king to be successfully attacked. So it is the opposing player's job to force a change in this position! That, in short, is the art of the king-side attack.

The following is another another sample game featuring Paul Morphy against an amateur. Don't get the wrong idea—Morphy played mostly against other grandmasters, and did quite well against them too. In fact, although there was no official world champion back in the mid-1800s, Morphy was known as the "first unofficial world champion." He beat every great player of his day, except for one—Howard **Staunton**, an Englishman, for whom the modern standard set of chess pieces is named. Yes, he's the same guy who invented the "English opening" we saw before. Staunton wisely stayed on his side of the Atlantic Ocean and managed to avoid ever playing Morphy! Although Morphy retired from the game when he was still young, he is even today regarded as one of the best, and most exciting, players of all time, which is why we keep turning to his games as examples.

The game below happens to be a perfect example of a king-side attack, coming out of an opening we're already familiar with. It's also a classic example of Paul Morphy's chess-playing style:

PAUL MORPHY (WHITE) VS. AMATEUR PLAYER (BLACK)

GIUOCO PIANO OPENING

1. **e4...e5**
2. **Nf3...Nc6**
3. **Bc4...Bc5**
4. **b4...Bxb4**
5. **c3...Ba5** (a slightly different move from the one in the last game)

6. d4...ed

7. 0-0...dc

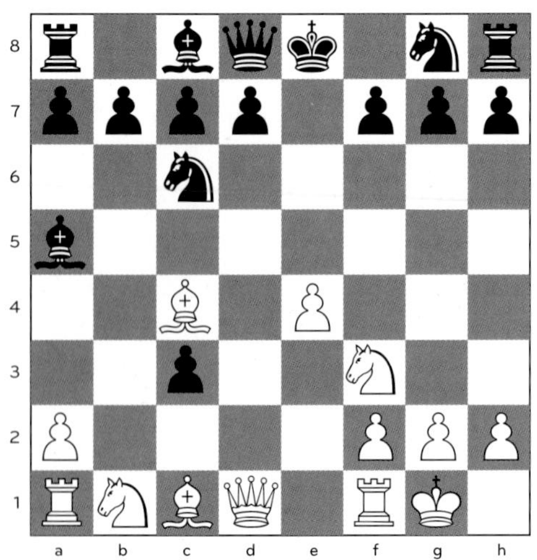

Now we'll see what happens after Black greedily grabs that extra pawn:

8. Ba3...

Morphy prevents Black from protecting his king by castling, since the f8 square is now attacked by the White bishop on a3.

8. ...d6

9. Qb3!...

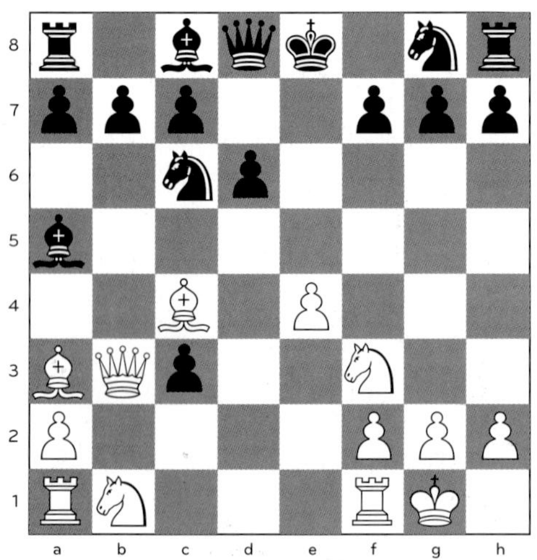

Morphy now is attacking Black's king side on two diagonals—a2 to g8 and a3 to f8—and is threatening to completely open up the game with e5, forcing the second diagonal open and also opening the e file to white's rook. Black knows he'd better do something to protect his king before it's too late.

9. ...Nh6

10. Nxc3...Bxc3

11. Qxc3...0-0

12. Rad1... (meaning that the rook on the a file moves to d1. This puts pressure on the pawn at d6, threatening to take complete control of the d file for White.)

12. ...Ng4

Black is trying to protect the e5 square from White's pawn advance.

13. h3...Nge5 (meaning that the knight on the g file moves to e5)

14. Nxe5...Nxe5

15. Be2...

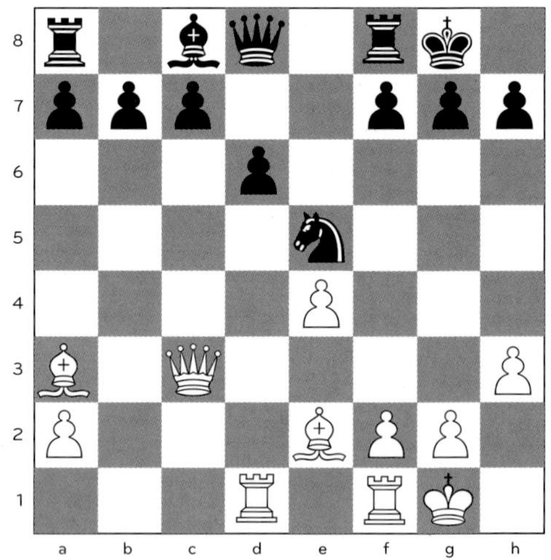

At this point, White is down by two pawns, but has the positional advantage. His pieces move freely on the queen side, aiming their firepower at Black's king. Black's pieces are mostly stuck on the back rank and pose no threat of counterattack.

15. ...f5?

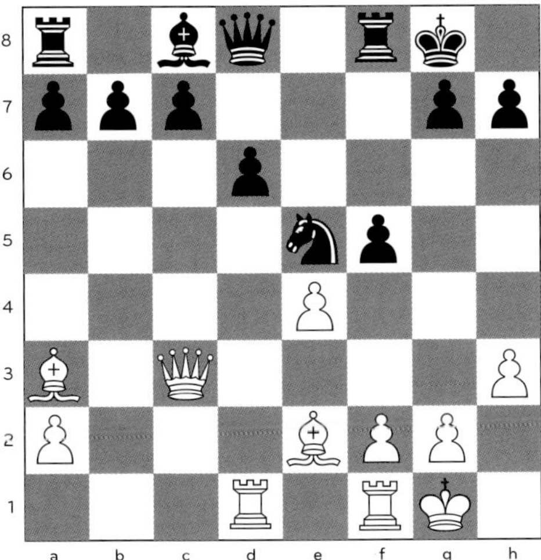

This is a critical mistake for Black. This opens the board further, which at this point can only help White. Because he is better developed, Morphy can beat Black to the punch by forcing open the e file and controlling it, as well as the a1 to h8 and a2 to g8 diagonals. A better move for Black would have been **15. ...f6**.

16. f4...Nc6 (a safe move, but out of the action)

17. Bc4+...Kh8

18. Bb2...Qe7 (Black protects the pawn on g7 and stalls a checkmate.)

19. Rde1...Rf6

20. ef...Qf8

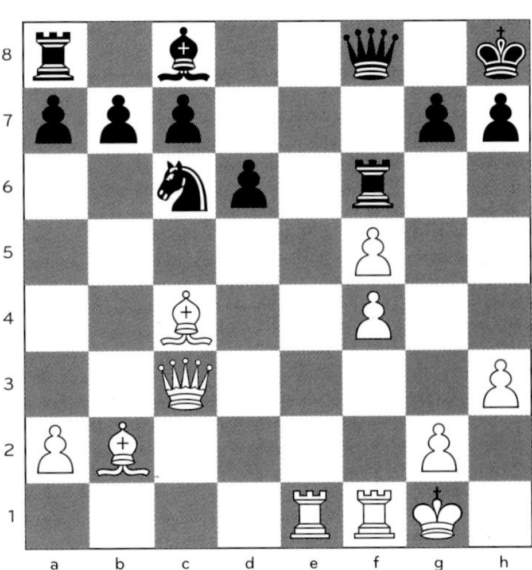

White is now ready to deliver the final blow. Remember, only sacrifice when it brings you some benefit—as it surely does here!

21. Re8...Qxe8

22. Qxf6! (if **gxf6** then **Bxf6#!**)**...Qe7**

Black is offering to exchange queens here, but White is not interested. Instead, he makes an even bigger sacrifice:

23. Qxg7+!...Qxg7

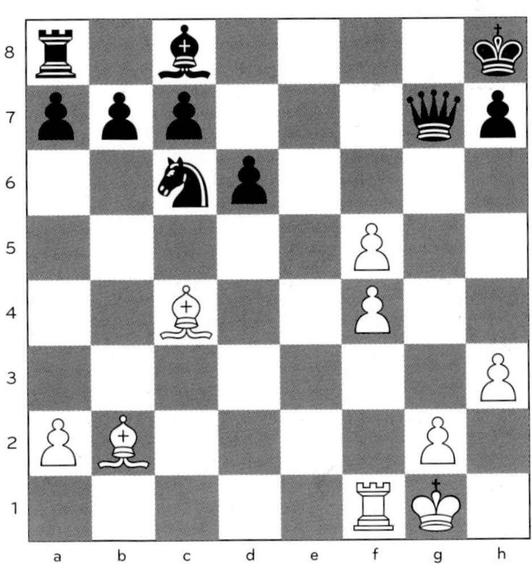

Will White capture Black's queen with his bishop? No—he's got an even better move up his sleeve:

24. f6!!...

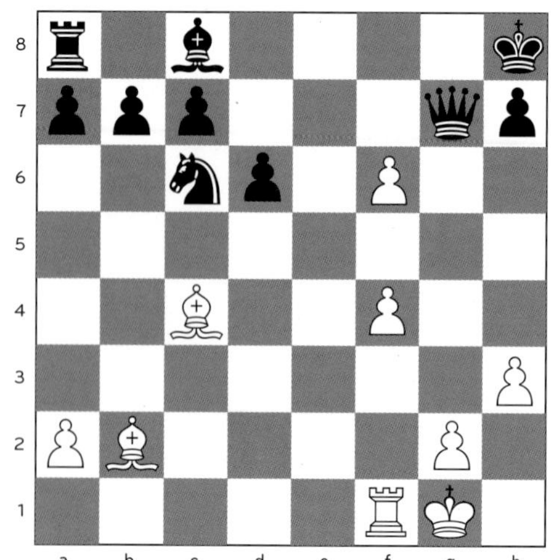

Black resigns here because he knows that there's no point in continuing. Here's what would have happened if he did:

24. ...Qf8

25. f7+ (discovered check, see page 42) **...Ne5**

26. fxe5...h5 (if Black takes White's pawn here, it's checkmate with **Bxe5#!**)

27. e6+ (another discovered check!) **...Kh7**

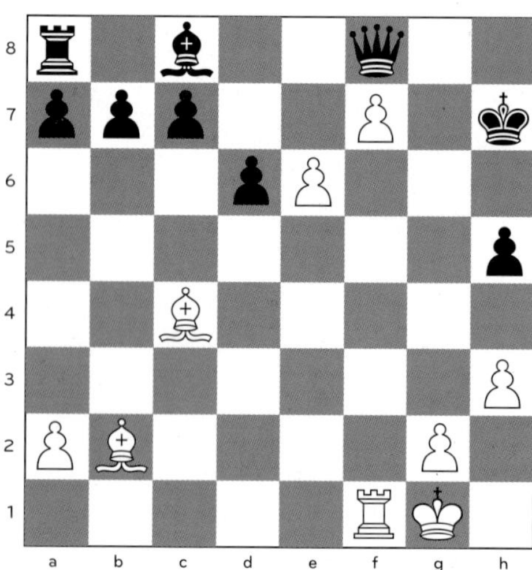

28. Bd3+...Kh6
29. Rf6+...Kg5
30. Rg6+...Kf4
31. Kf2!

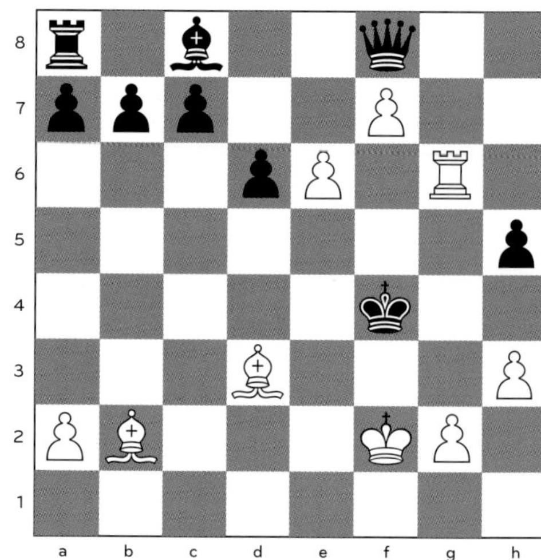

No matter what move Black makes here, the next move for White ends things with **g3#!**

CHESS PROBLEMS FROM THE MIDDLE GAME

You can find the answers on page 113.

PROBLEM 1

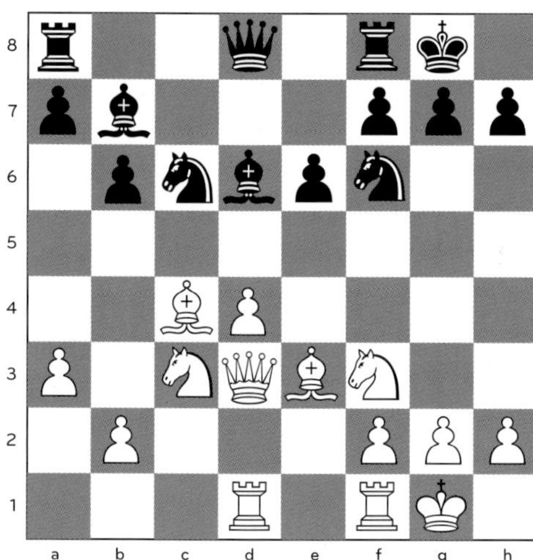

This is a typical isolated queen pawn middle game. What plan can you recommend for White? What pieces should White try to trade?

PROBLEM 2

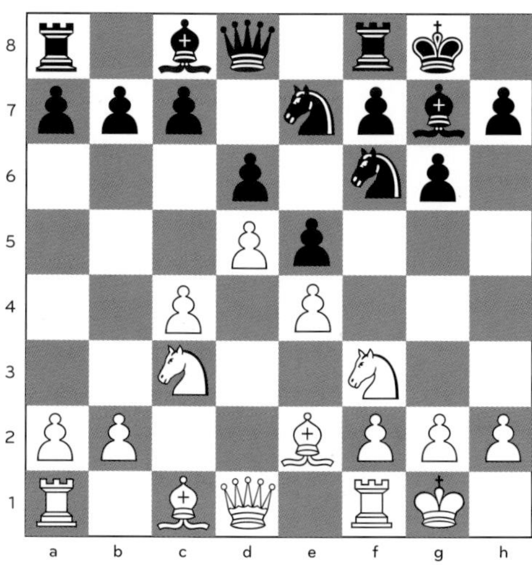

Black has greater central influence on the King-side where **e5** has already been played. White has more space on the Queen-side where **d5** has been played. On which side of the board should each side focus their attacks?

PROBLEM 3

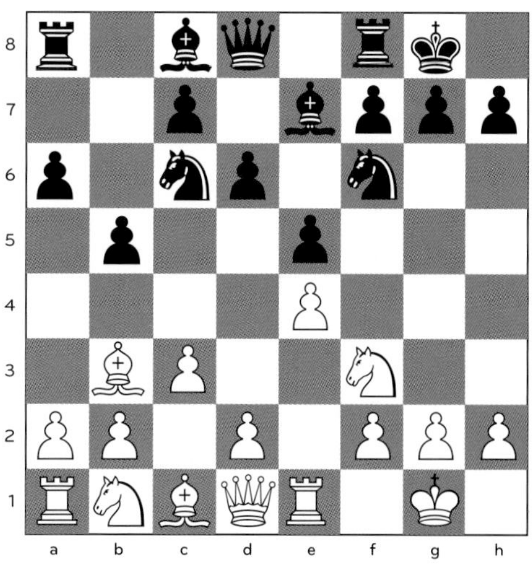

Here is a typical closed Ruy Lopez middle game. White wants to control the center by playing **d4**. However, he doesn't want Black to prevent his control of the d4 square with **...Bg4**. What should be White's preparatory move? How might Black then respond?

PROBLEM 4

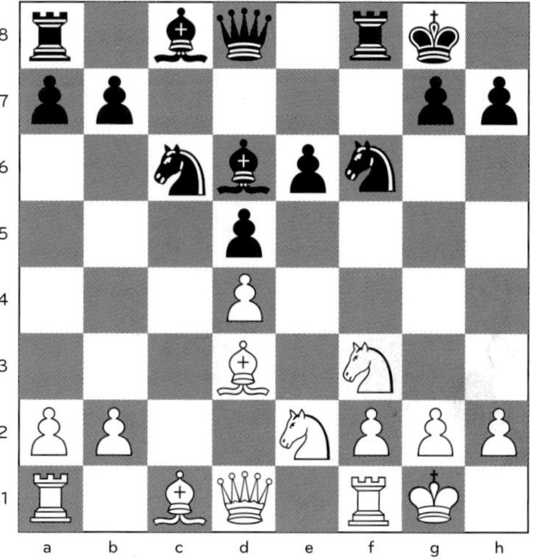

Black has a weak square on e5 and a backward pawn on e6. Black has some freedom, though, by having an open f-file. White should make moves to neutralize that freedom while trying to keep Black's central pawns and squares weak. What can White play here to prevent Black from playing **...e5**?

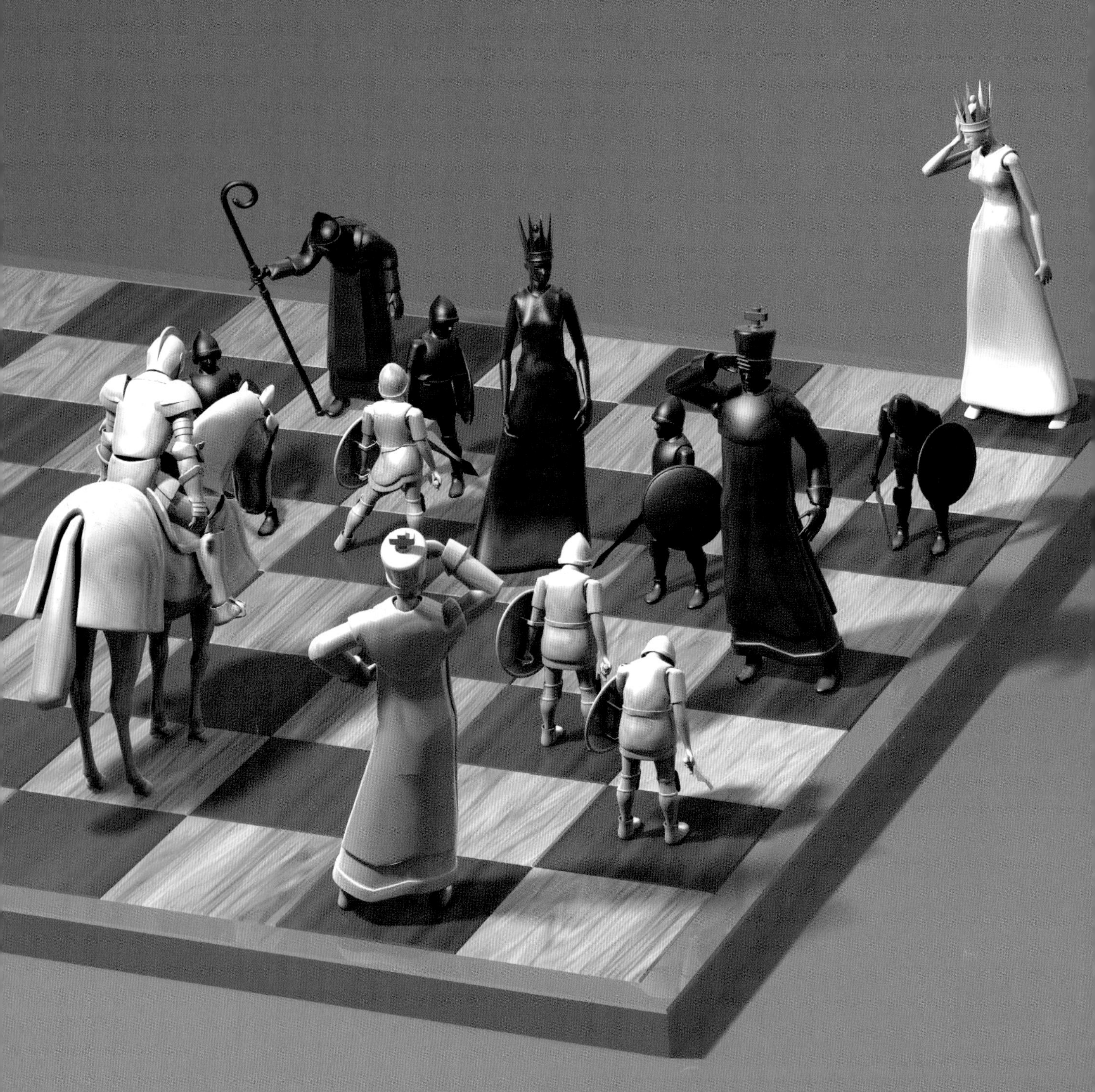

CHAPTER FIVE

THE ENDGAME

THE WAR HAS BEEN BRUTAL AND PUNISHING. YOUR troops have engaged in fierce battle, maneuvered long and hard, attacked and defended, sacrificed and captured. And still, neither side has been triumphant. Now the remains of the two armies are spread thinly across the wide-open spaces of the battlefield, ready to fight on till the last one standing has declared victory!

Welcome to the endgame, General.

PLAYING THE ENDGAME

Having only a couple of pieces doesn't mean the game will end in a draw—not at all! You can win a game with a king and a single pawn if all your opponent has left is his king. That's right; it's time to use that special move you've been waiting all game to play: the pawn promotion. If you can get that lowly pawn to the back rank, you can make it a queen!

PASSED PAWNS

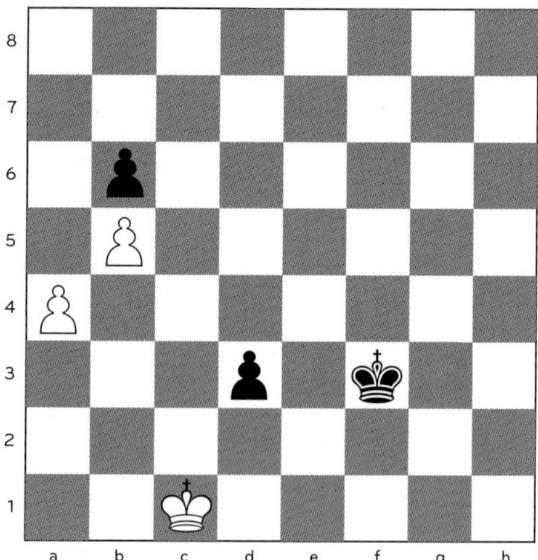

Here, Black has a **passed pawn**, one that has no enemy pawn in its way. Having a passed pawn is a great advantage in chess, especially in the endgame. Black can now maneuver to convert his pawn to a queen, ensuring his victory. Can you see how?

Black's pawn on d3 has no White pawn that can stop it. However, White's king is close enough to potentially get in its way on the way to the promoting square. Black's king can help his passed pawn.

COUNTING SQUARES
When you have a passed pawn, and all the opponent has to stop you with is his king, how can you figure out if you can make it to the back rank to convert your pawn? Here's how: Count the squares from your pawn to the back rank. Now count the squares from your pawn to the opponent's king. If the second number is greater, you're all set. If it's the same or less than the first number, you can't win that race!

1. ...Ke2! And Black's next two moves will be to advance the passed pawn to get a queen.

1. ...Ke3 doesn't work. It would lead to **2. Kd1!...d2 3. a5!...bxa5 4. b6**, and White now has a passed pawn that will promote before either of Black's passed pawns.

Even in the opening and throughout the middle game, look to create passed pawns for yourself and deny them to your opponent.

HERE COMES THE KING!

The king is not a very powerful piece. He's slow moving and needs to be protected. Still, he can come in handy at the end of a game, when most of the more powerful and dangerous pieces have been taken off the board. That's when you'll want him out there in the thick of the battle. In fact, to achieve

victory in the endgame, it's vital to get your king involved. He may have been more vulnerable than powerful till now, but when there aren't many pieces and pawns left, each one becomes much more important.

Sometimes, it takes many moves for the king to reach the square you're aiming at, but your opponent is most likely in the same situation. Never mind hiding your king behind a protective wall—that wall is long gone by the endgame, and it's vital to throw every piece or pawn you have left into the battle.

In fact, although the sample games in this book are relatively short, there are chess games that last 50, 60, even 100 moves! Since endgame moves tend to be made by kings and pawns (often the only ones left), which go one square at a time, it can take a lot of moves.

ENDGAME STRATEGY AND TACTICS

We won't go into this piece by piece like the other sections because by this point you're likely to have only a few pieces left.

Here are some key things to remember about the endgame.

Get your king into the action. He can serve to protect pawns and shepherd them into the final rank where they can be converted. He can also attack enemy pawns, especially if they're isolated or backward.

Maneuver yourself into some passed pawns and try to advance and promote them. If you're ahead in number of pawns, try to stay ahead. Exchange other pieces instead. It's only the pawns that can be converted to game-changing pieces. Try to keep your pawns linked so that they can protect each other. Avoid isolated pawns, but if they belong to your opponent, attack them!

If you're ahead in material or position, try to trade as many pieces and pawns as possible to get to a simpler board. That way, your opponent will run out of material before you do.

If you're falling behind, resist material exchanges, and try to trap your opponent into a mistake that lets you draw the game instead of losing (see the first Morphy game example, page 72). Your goal in this case is to keep from losing everything but your king. If you can hold your pieces out long enough, you may be able to force your opponent into a critical mistake.

All it takes is having your king one square closer to a key square than your opponent's king. If you can get there first, you can convert a pawn, or stop your opponent from doing so, or perhaps you can capture a weak pawn before your opponent gets there to defend it.

Block your opponent's passed pawns as best you can, although it may be difficult and requires you to divert your forces from other tasks. Your king can be helpful in blocking passed pawns, but it is more important to keep him in a protected position than it is for your other pieces. Prevent your opponent from promoting his pawns at all costs! Knights are the best blockers of passed pawns because they can also jump over the passed pawn they're blocking in order to capture another opposing piece or pawn. Rooks are also useful for blocking passed pawns because they can cover entire ranks and files at the same time. This is a huge advantage in the endgame, when the board has wide-open spaces.

When you've got an advantage, try to maneuver the opposing king into the corner where he can be checkmated or isolated from the rest of the action. This can be done with your rooks, bishops, knights, queen, or even your king. It may take time for your king to overtake your opponent's king since it can only move one square at a time. But this is also true for your opponent's

king. It may take a while, but a king can still do the job!

When both sides have bishops on the same color, the player with the material advantage should look to trade the two bishops for each other. This will preserve your advantage in material (or position) and remove an annoying obstacle to your remaining pawns.

In the endgame, a rook is much stronger than a bishop or knight because it can cover both ranks and files at the same time. One rook can block the entire back rank, stopping your opponent from converting his pawns on any file (unless the pawn has backup protection from other pieces).

MATING PATTERNS

As you improve at the game of chess, you'll find yourself recognizing patterns in the games you play, as well as in the ones you follow through notation. Although every chess game is different, they do tend to follow certain patterns, especially in the opening, but also during combinations of moves that result in checkmate.

There are many of these mating patterns, far too many to list here. But here are a few, just so you get the idea of what to look for. Mating patterns are things you want to repeat, so long as it's *you* doing the mating!

BACK-RANK MATES

Here, White's king is on his back rank, with a wall of three pawns protecting him. Of course, they're also *blocking* him from moving. When Black brings her rook down to a1, it's checkmate! Remember to give your king an escape hatch by advancing your pawn to h3 well before

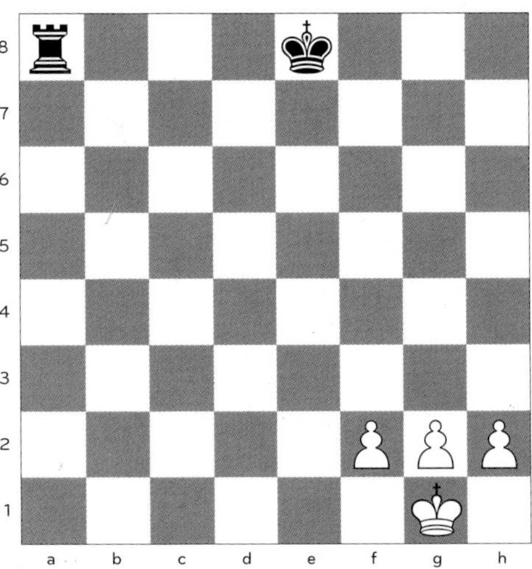

your opponent's rook is in position to attack you. And if you're on the attacking side, if your opponent's king can be trapped on his back rank, and you've developed your rook so that it is on an open file, remember this pattern and deliver the fatal blow!

QUEEN AND HELPER MATES

The powerful queen needs the help of at least one pawn or piece to deliver a checkmate. Typically, the attacking pawn or piece is deep in enemy territory, helping to prevent the opponent's king from escaping.

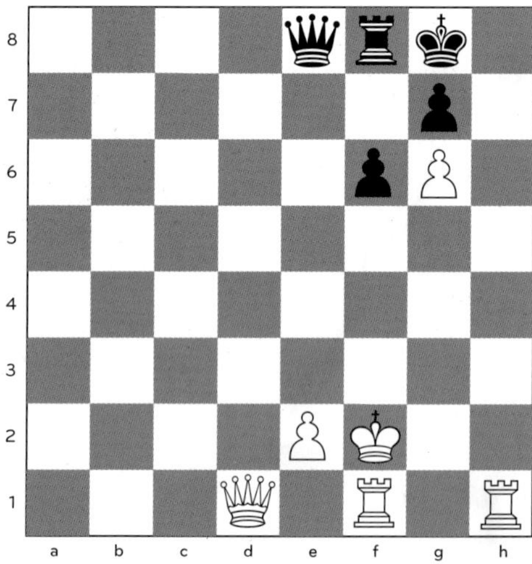

This common mate has the name of Damiano's Mate because it was first discussed by Pedro Damiano, a Portuguese chess player, in a book he had published in 1512. Here, White's pawn is at g6, keeping Black's king from moving either to f7 or h7. The f8 square is occupied by Black's rook, which got there when Black castled. The h file is open for White's rook to attack. Notice that White's king has cleared his back rank, freeing it for the other rook and the queen to join the attack. To achieve mate, White needs to get his queen to h7. How can he do it? By sacrificing both his rooks, one after the other!

1. **Rh8!...Kxh8**
2. **Rh1+...Kg8**
3. **Rh8+!...Kxh8**
4. **Qh1+...Kg8**
5. **Qh7#!**

This is a devilishly clever combination involving a brilliant double sacrifice. It succeeded because White was able to see a full four moves ahead of his rival. From the moment he makes his first move, Black has no choice but to respond to White's moves, rather than sway the game in his favor.

QUEEN AND KNIGHT MATES

The queen and her knight make a grand pair for a checkmate. They work so well together because their powers are different, and between them, they can make almost every move there is on a chessboard. Here's a classic example:

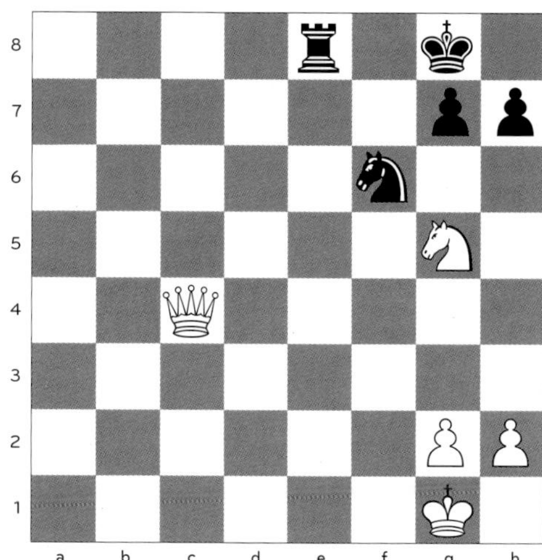

Black is in check from White's queen. He can put his rook in the way with Re6, but that doesn't do much good, since the queen takes it and Black is still in the same situation. So he can either move his king to f8 or h8. If he moves to f8, White's queen checkmates him with Qf7#. So Black has no better move than Kh8. White responds with Nf7, forcing Black's king back to where it began, with Kg8. White then moves Nh6+! Black can't take the White knight with his pawn, because he has to use his turn to escape check. Again, if he moves to f8, White's queen delivers mate with Qf7, protected by the White knight as before. So Black moves Kh8 again. Only this time, unlike before, White's knight is in position to force mate with Qg8#!!

ZUGZWANG

Zugzwang (from the German, meaning "forced to move") is a very bad position to be in. When you are in Zugzwang, you may not be in any danger in your current position—the problem is, you have to make a move, and there's no place to move that doesn't get you in trouble! Stay out of Zugzwang and try to get your opponent into it!

Black is in Zugzwang. Anywhere he moves, he pays a heavy price because White will be able to advance his pawn to f8 and convert it to a queen! Too bad you can't pass in chess—you have to move when it's your turn.

STOUT

CHAPTER SIX

THE WIDE WORLD OF CHESS

By now, you've probably played a few actual games of chess, as well as followed along through the tutorial games in this book. You can see how chess gets your competitive juices flowing! Well, after a while, as you improve, you may find yourself ahead of the local competition, your friends and classmates. You may even want to challenge yourself by entering a **tournament** and seeing how you stack up to the competition.

World chess champions, shown clockwise from top left: Alexander Alekhine, Boris Spassky playing Bobby Fischer, Jose-Raoul Capablanca playing Emanuel Lasker, Anatoly Karpov, and Mikhail Botvinnik

TOURNAMENT CHESS

THERE ARE THREE KINDS OF TOURNAMENTS

Matches are between two players only. Until recently, in world championship matches, the players faced off in game after game until one player reached a certain score (victories are counted as 1 point, draws as ½ half point, and losses as 0 points). After the longest world championship chess match in history, between Anatoly Karpov and Garry Kasparov in 1984–1985 (see page 95), new rules were put in place to limit the length of matches for the world crown. Now, a specific length is agreed upon before the match begins.

Round-robin tournaments are ones in which every player plays against every other player who has entered into the tournament, and the player with the best results wins, or the two best players move on to a final round.

Most tournaments you'll encounter will use the **Swiss System**. Here, players are ranked according to their **FIDE** (for international tournaments) or **USCF** (for U.S. tournaments) ratings, and the weakest play the strongest first. Then, the losers of the first game are separated from the winners into a group, and these two separate groups pair their players up the same way for the next game. This continues, so as the tournament goes on, the stronger players are playing against stronger competition and the weaker players face each other.

If you do enter a tournament, there are a few things to know first. We've already explained the touch-move rule. While your family or friends may let you take back a bad move, when you play people you don't know in a competitive tournament, touch move is the law of the land. There are a few other tournament basics to get used to as well:

TIMERS

Tick . . . tick . . . tick. Get ready for that sound, because once you start playing tournament chess, you'll be hearing a lot of it. In most chess tournaments, you only get a certain amount of time to make a certain number of moves. It's not that every individual move has a time limit. You can still sit there for a while thinking over all the possibilities. But every minute you spend on a move is one less minute to spend later on when you may need the extra time even more!

Before 1883, when clocks were first used, it was common for games to last eight hours—even all day! Players could take as long as they wanted to for each move—and many did.

Today, the normal time limit for tournaments is two hours (each player) for 40 moves. But this can vary, because the organizers of each tournament are free to set their own time limits, and school tournaments generally feature even shorter time frames.

The introduction of strict time limits has changed the world of tournament chess. If you divide two hours by 40 moves, it comes out to three minutes per move, per player. However, if you use three minutes for each of your early moves, you will be in big trouble when the real action begins. That's why it's so important to know the ideas and themes of as many of the standard openings as you can.

If you already know what to do early in the game, you can save a lot of time with your first moves. Every second you save may be the second that saves *you* later on: the instant when you see the fatal flaw in your opponent's defense, or the second you notice a weakness of your own that you need to fix.

Now, back to that awful ticking sound. . . .

The first **chess clock** was invented in England in 1883, and they have been plaguing tournament players ever since. Some clocks are silent—but trust us—you'll hear that ticking in your head anyway. Try to stay calm, though. The idea is for you to save more time for later than your opponent is doing. How? By keeping your opponent off-balance, making him think for a while before making each move, costing him precious seconds and priceless minutes. If you succeed in this, he is much more likely to make a mistake when the battle action is thickest and he must make critical choices; he might even have to forfeit the game if he runs out of time altogether!

Remember: Time can be your enemy or your friend. In tournament chess, preparation means success!

CLUBS AND RATINGS

The first chess clubs were founded in Italy around the year 1550. They are still around today, and if you really get into the game, you may enjoy being part of a club near you. Clubs are a great way to get to know other serious players and to improve your game. Chess clubs and chess cafés, where you can snack and sip while you play, are also great places to pick up equipment like chessboards, chess sets, clocks, books, and computer programs.

Most tournaments are organized by local chess clubs or by national federations, like the United States Chess Federation, or USCF. In Great Britain, it's the British Chess Association/British Chess Federation **(BCA/BCF)** that does the organizing. International tournaments that feature players from all over the world are run by the International Chess Federation, or FIDE, its French initials, which stand for Fédération Internationale des Échecs. USCF, BCA/BCF, and FIDE all have slightly different tournament rules, but as far as the basics go, they're the same.

Your "seeding," or ranking, in a tournament will depend on your chess **rating**. Rating is determined by your official record in previous tournament games. Every player is given a certain point score, and that score determines your rating. You get your score by playing in tournaments against other rated players. Until you've played in one, you are considered unrated.

Players with a rating of 2,300 points or higher are considered FIDE **chess masters**. Those who have done well in tournaments against other masters can graduate to the level of **international master** and, ultimately, the highest level of all: grandmaster.

Currently, FIDE does not rate players lower than 1,400. USCF ratings, on the other hand, cover a much wider ground, with the lowest possible rating being 100. There are several classes below master:

200–399	=	Class I
400–599	=	Class H
600–799	=	Class G
800–999	=	Class F
1,000–1,199	=	Class E
1,200–1,399	=	Class D
1,400–1,599	=	Class C
1,600–1,799	=	Class B
1,800–1,999	=	Class A
2,000–2,199	=	Expert
2,200–2,399	=	Master
2,400 and up	=	Senior Master

TOURNAMENT TIPS

When you enter a tournament, you cannot assume they will have enough equipment for every player. It's wise to bring your own chessboard, set of pieces, and chess clock.

Clocks are either analog, with two faces (one for you and one for your opponent), or digital, in which case there are two digital clock readouts. After your move, you hit a button on your side of the clock, which stops your clock and starts your opponent's. When he is done with his move, he hits the button on his side of the clock, and it's back to you.

RESIGNING WITH CLASS

For beginners, it's best to play every game of chess out to the bitter end because you can always learn something from every move. But as you get to be a better player, and especially when you play in tournaments, chess etiquette demands a timely end to a game that is basically over.

So, unless you're a real beginner, when you see that you have no hope of winning or drawing, there's no point in dragging out the game. It's good sportsmanship to know when and how to **resign**.

Don't sweep all the pieces off the board in anger. Don't smash your fist down on the board or trash-talk your opponent. Simply take your king and lay him on his side, and then stand up and offer your hand in congratulations. This may not feel so great, but on the plus side, you can expect the same behavior in return when you're the winner.

When you are playing in a tournament, use good chess manners at all times. Be still and silent when it's your opponent's turn and even when it's your own turn. Don't eat at the chess table, and don't keep getting up and down. In general, behave the way you would want your opponent to behave, and hope he or she does the same for you. By exhibiting proper chess etiquette, you'll be following in the footsteps of none other than Benjamin Franklin, who wrote the first book on chess etiquette way back in the 1700s!

CHANGES AND CHAMPIONS: MILESTONES OF THE MODERN GAME

Even though chess in its modern form has been played for longer than 500 years, the first formal chess tournament wasn't held until 1575, in Madrid, Spain. Ever since then, players have been competing with each other to see who's best. In 1851, the first international tournament was held. It was won by Adolf Anderssen of Germany.

The first Official World Championship took place in 1886. The winner was Wilhelm Steinitz, an Austrian American, who defeated Johannes Herman Zukertort of Poland. Steinitz was declared the first Official World Champion of Chess. From that time on, there has always been a world champion, and sometimes even two competing world champions!

Here is the complete list:

UNDISPUTED CHAMPIONS

Wilhelm Steinitz: 1886–1894
Emanuel Lasker: 1894–1921
Jose-Raoul Capablanca: 1921–1927
Alexander Alekhine: 1927–1935, 1937–1946
Max Euwe: 1935–1937
Mikhail Botvinnik: 1948–1957, 1958–1960, 1961–1963
Vassily Smyslov: 1957–1958
Mikhail Tal: 1960–1961
Tigran Petrosian: 1963–1969
Boris Spassky: 1969–1972
Bobby Fischer: 1972–1975
Anatoly Karpov: 1975–1985
Garry Kasparov: 1985–1993
Vladimir Kramnik: 2006–2007
Viswanathan Anand: 2008–present

DISPUTED CHAMPIONS

(From 1993 to 2008, there were always two rival champions, sanctioned by rival chess organizations. See page 94.)

FIDE

Anatoly Karpov: 1993–1999
Alexander Khalifman: 1999–2000
Viswanathan Anand: 2000–2002
Ruslan Ponomariov: 2002–2004
Rustan Kasimdzhanov: 2004–2005
Veselin Topalov: 2005–2006
Viswanathan Anand: 2007–2008

Classical World Champions

Garry Kasparov: 1993–2000
Vladimir Kramnik: 2000–2008

These players are the greatest in world history—well, at least in modern history. And there are some great stories that go along with their triumphs, some of which we'll tell you about. Chess championships don't take place on a regular schedule—FIDE, the world governing body of chess, holds them only when a worthy challenger emerges—and there can be gaps of several years between championship matches. When they do happen, the chess world is riveted for the weeks or months a match can take.

In 1993, then-champion Garry Kasparov broke away from FIDE to start his own world championship matches. From that time until 2006, when the competing titles were unified and the two organizations were reunited under FIDE, there were two world champions at a time!

In November 2008, Viswanathan Anand, of India, defeated the reigning World Champion Vladimir Kramnik, of Russia, to become the undisputed 15th Official World Chess Champion. In February 2009, Veselin Topalov, of Bulgaria, defeated Gata Kamsky, of the United States, to earn the right to challenge Anand for the World Championship. The match will likely take place in the spring of 2010, though the two camps are still in negotiations.

With the forming of FIDE in 1924, the world of championship chess was also opened to women. The first female world champion was Vera Menchik, who claimed the title in 1927. In recent years, female grandmasters like sisters Susan and Judith Polgar have emerged. For the first time, the world championship of chess is within the reach of players from both sexes.

Here is the list of female chess world champions. Most have been from the former Soviet Union or China:

Vera Menchik: 1927–1944
Lyudmila Rudenko: 1950–1953
Elisabeth Bykova: 1953–1956, 1958–1962
Olga Rubtsova: 1956–1958
Nona Gaprindashvili: 1962–1978
Maya Chiburdanidze: 1978–1991
Xie Jun: 1991–1996, 1999–2001
Susan Polgar: 1996–1999
Zhu Chen: 2001–2004
Antoaneta Stefanova: 2004–2006
Xu Yuhua: 2006–2007
Alexandra Kosteniuk: 2008–present

CHAMPIONSHIPS AND POLITICS

You may have noticed that many of the later champions have Russian-sounding names. In fact, from Botvinnik on, most champions have come from the former Soviet Union. Most were Russian, but Petrosian was from the Soviet Republic of Armenia, and the highest-rated player ever, Garry Kasparov, hails from the former Soviet Republic of Azerbaijan and is of Armenian-Jewish ancestry. Alexander Alekhine was Russian, but he fled the Soviet Union to live in Paris.

Chess became all the rage in the Soviet Union after the Russian Revolution of 1917. Lenin, the founder of the new union, was an avid player. He decided that the game of chess was ideal for promoting rational, methodical, modern thinking in his people. Josef Stalin, who ruled the

Soviet Union for more than 30 years after Lenin, also loved the game. In fact, he decided to prove to the entire world how the new communist system could produce better chess players, just as it could produce better Olympic athletes.

The Soviets' first big success was the championship of Mikhail Botvinnik, a loyal communist and a three-time champion. He was followed by a succession of Soviet players that was broken only in 1972 with the triumph of a young American chess phenomenon: Bobby Fischer. Fischer had blazed his way to the top of the chess world and was now in position to challenge world champion Boris Spassky, from the Soviet Union, of course.

The Fischer–Spassky championship match was the most closely watched chess match in history. People all over the world left work early to watch the games and analysis on television. The match stood as a symbol of the Cold War then going on between the Soviet Union and the U.S. Fischer, a brilliant but troubled young man, was hugely popular in America as he went up against the champion, Spassky. Fischer won, turning the world of chess upside down. People were calling him the "best player ever," and perhaps he was, and would have remained world champion for a long time. But shortly after he won the title, Fischer went into seclusion and refused to defend his title or play championship chess again. FIDE took away his title in 1975 and awarded it to Anatoly Karpov of the Soviet Union who had won the most recent qualifying tournament to decide who would get to challenge Fischer. Fischer stayed away from competitive chess for another 20 years. In spite of being recognized as one of the top 10 players of all time, he never played for another world championship.

Garry Kasparov, the legendary chess player who we've mentioned a few times already, was a vocal critic of the Soviet regime. He faced off against Soviet favorite and then world champion Anatoly Karpov in an epic championship match in Moscow, Russia, in 1984. The match was set up so that the first player to record six victories would be declared the champion. Kasparov jumped out to a quick lead, but was unable to keep the advantage over a series of long, agonizing games. Audiences even began to boo

Garry Kasparov stares down Anatoly Karpov in the 1985 World Chess Championship in Moscow.

when the players took too long to make a move. As their nerves began to fray, each player accused the other of using dirty tricks to "psych out" his opponent. Finally, after many, many draws, it began to look as if Kasparov would eventually outlast Karpov and win the championship. That was when the Soviet Sports Federation, which was running the match, stepped in to suspend play, saving the exhausted Karpov from defeat after 17 straight draws! The following year, the match was restarted from the beginning, after a five-month layoff. As expected, Kasparov won and claimed the world title, which he held until the year 2000. In 2002, he retired from competitive chess.

PSYCH OUT!

Way back in the 1500s, the chess-playing monk Ruy Lopez tried to "psych out" his opponents by playing them late in the afternoon and positioning the board so that the sun was shining right into their eyes. He was probably not the first to use such tactics, and he was certainly not the last. Chess players have long since learned how to get inside their opponents' heads, making them lose concentration just when they need it the most. They may stare at their opponent constantly, or giggle at an opponent's move, causing them to doubt their wisdom. They may start clearing their throat, or coughing, or humming, or drumming their fingers on the table, or just shifting in their chair when it's the opponent's turn to move. All this distraction can cost an opponent valuable time and concentration. Of course, this is bad behavior, and goes against chess manners, but that doesn't mean it doesn't happen.

In tournaments, the time element and the competition raise the tension level. Since players aren't supposed to talk to one another during the game, except to offer a draw, the room is very quiet. The smallest noise or movement can get in the way of a player's focus. Nowhere is this "mental game" of chess more noticeable than during world championship matches, when millions of people worldwide are following every move, and the pressure is at its greatest.

In 1977, during a world championship match between Anatoly Karpov and challenger Viktor Korchnoi, the psych-outs reached new heights of absurdity. Karpov was, as we've said, from the Soviet Union. So was Korchnoi, but he had left for the West two years before and had spoken out against the Soviet communist system. This match had huge political meaning.

During the second game, one of his assistants brought Karpov a container of yogurt. Afterward, Korchnoi complained that this was a secret signal, part of a prearranged code depending on when it was offered and, perhaps, the flavor of the yogurt. After tense negotiations, it was determined that Karpov could indeed have his mid-game snack, but it could be brought to him only after the twentieth move of each game and had to be the same flavor every time!

And that wasn't all! In a direct effort to psych out the challenger, a Soviet "mind reader" sent by his government sat in the crowd, staring straight at Korchnoi from the start of the match to its finish. Not surprisingly, Karpov won. Too bad he didn't fight fair and square!

FAMOUS CHESS SCAMS

In 1769, a new contestant entered the picture: the Automaton Turk, a chess-playing machine created by the Hungarian nobleman Baron Wolfgang von Kempelen. It began touring Europe and the United States, taking on challengers and defeating almost all of them. Among its victims were said to be Napoleon and Benjamin Franklin. A mechanical man with a Turkish headdress appeared to move the pieces. But the Automaton Turk was really no machine at all—it had a secret compartment where a chess master hid, making all the moves by pulling the automaton's levers. The fiendish fake lasted until 1854, when it was unmasked and destroyed.

But that was not the end of chess scams for all time. In 1878, Mephisto, a "chess-playing automaton" designed by Englishman Charles Godfrey Gumpel, appeared in London to the amazement of its audience, which by then had forgotten the very existence of the Automaton Turk. Of course, this machine, like the Turk, contained a real chess player hiding inside it.

EXHIBITION CHESS

In addition to holding tournaments and regular matches for members, chess clubs often host visiting or member grandmasters, who put on exhibitions for the entertainment of an audience of avid casual players (called kibitzers) who love to discuss great games during and afterward. These exhibitions can simply be matches between two great players, or they can take other, more exotic forms:

LIVING CHESS

Back in the Middle Ages, someone got the bright idea of playing chess on a really big board, with real people substituting for the pawns and pieces! Of course, there had to be something in the way of hats or clothing to indicate which piece or pawn each person stood for. Living chess is something you rarely see, but it still goes on, which proves that it must be fun!

LIGHTNING CHESS

Lightning chess is a game in which each player has only a very short amount of time to move. It's also called speed chess or **blitz chess**. Typically, each player has only five minutes of time to complete the game! Want to get even more extreme? Try bullet chess: Each player gets only *one minute* to complete all his moves in the game!

SIMULTANEOUS CHESS

In **simultaneous chess**, a great player plays several games at once against different opponents. Only the best players can concentrate on several different positions in turn, and without losing focus.

BLINDFOLD CHESS

Blindfold chess is when a skilled player plays one or more games at once with his or her eyes covered and usually wins most of them! The ability to keep positions, sometimes more than one, in your

head as the game progresses is an amazing feat. Try it yourself one day if you think it's easy! Nowadays, actual blindfolds are rare. The master or grandmaster who is playing will simply turn his back to the chessboards, however many there are. The official record for most simultaneous blindfold chess games is held by the American grandmaster George Koltanowski, who played 34 games at once back in 1934!

EXTRA, EXTRA, READ ALL ABOUT IT!

A great way to improve your chess game is to play out the **annotated** games that are featured in most newspapers at least once a week. These usually come with commentary by the editor. The first newspaper column featuring chess games appeared in 1813. If you can find such a column in your local paper, you can start to build up your own collection of great games. Playing through and analyzing these games can help you recognize patterns, avoid blunders, and give you ideas for ingenious attacks!

CHESS PROBLEMS

Sometimes, the newspaper chess column will feature **chess problems** as well. These are puzzles that offer you the chance to jump into the middle of a game, in a situation where finding the right move will win it for you. Here are two examples of chess problems, with the answers printed at the back of the book. See if you can solve them yourself! (For solutions, see page 113.)

PROBLEM 1: ADMIRED BY LENIN

This problem was said to have been a favorite of Vladimir Lenin.

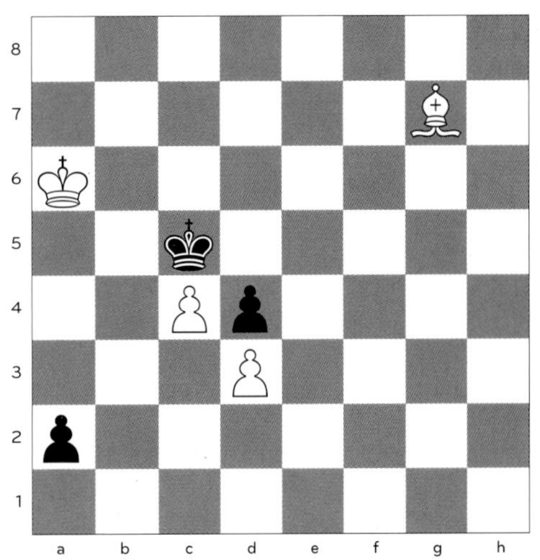

What is White's winning move?

PROBLEM 2: SMYTH VS. HELMS

This game was played between Samuel Smyth as White and Herman Helms as Black.

White is up by a rook minus a pawn—a large material advantage. But Black is on the attack. What move can he make to force checkmate in two moves?

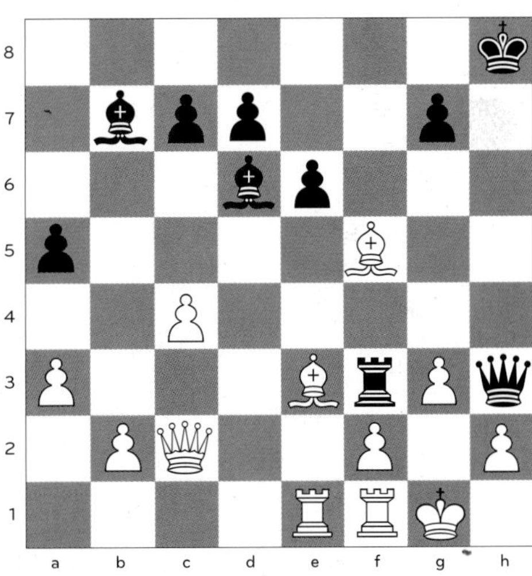

COMPUTERS AND CHESS

Of course, if you're tired of beating your parents and your friends, and your local newspaper doesn't have a chess column, you can always choose to play a non-human opponent: the computer. There are several fine programs you can buy or download if you don't already have one that came with the computer when you bought it.

The first true chess software was invented in the 1950s by a computer pioneer named Alan Turing. From the earliest days of computer science, chess was looked at as one of the ideal ways to apply and develop artificial intelligence. Scientists believed that if they could design a program that could play chess the way a human does, it would help them understand how the human mind worked, which in turn would help them design better, more powerful and useful computers.

But that's not how it turned out in the real world. Humans, it seems, reason in very complex ways. A human chess player looks for patterns and tries to find weaknesses in his opponent's position and thinking, as well as his psychological makeup. A computer is merely a fixed system that performs how its human programmer wants it to perform.

It turned out that what computers were really good at was crunching millions of numbers really fast. Where a human could look two or three moves ahead, a computer could quickly analyze

and calculate millions of possible chess positions, assign each one a numerical rating, and then make the move with the highest rating.

Improvements in computing speed and power resulted over time in computers that could play chess well enough to challenge the greatest human players. These days, even your home computer can run chess programs that can beat almost any human most of the time. Still, apart from their calculating abilities, computers have yet to reach the level of complexity of the human brain.

GRANDMASTER VS. GIGABYTE

The first chess computers weren't very fast, but soon they picked up speed. By 1982, a computer named Belle by its inventor Ken Thompson earned the rating of master in a U.S. tournament. Then, in 1989, a computer named Deep Blue, designed by a team of IBM engineers, challenged Garry Kasparov, then world champion and widely considered the best chess player, to an exhibition match.

The world held its breath. Surely no computer could beat the great Kasparov! And sure enough, Kasparov won the match easily. Again in 1996, he beat the computer handily. But that didn't spell the end of chess computers—far from it! The IBM team went back to work, retooled Deep Blue, and challenged Kasparov again in May 1997. This time, after five games, the match was tied. Everything rode on the sixth and final game.

Kasparov, as confident as anyone who has ever played the game, began to doubt himself. Deep Blue, which was after all only a machine, had no such doubts. Perhaps that is why it was able to defeat its human opponent, proving once and for all that chess computers had come of age. Kasparov was so angry that he refused to accept defeat. "In a regular tournament," he shouted, "I would tear it to pieces!"

These days, you can go to a chess club or a computer store and buy a database containing millions of games played by top players all over the world. You can access them at any time, and learn from them as you play out the games. In fact, it's hard to find a chess professional these days who doesn't carry a laptop containing such a database for reference.

LONG-DISTANCE COMBAT

CORRESPONDENCE CHESS

For centuries (ever since chess notation was invented), people have been playing chess by mail, also known as **correspondence chess**. Of course, in the old days, some of these games lasted quite a long time. Letters had to be mailed and carried by horse, train, truck, or plane to wherever in the world the other player was—back and forth with every move! Thank goodness, nowadays there's e-mail. Better yet, you can play real, live long-distance opponents in real time.

INTERNET CHESS

Care to play a real-live opponent, but can't find anyone handy? No problem! These days, you can always find an opponent ready to play, day or night, via the Internet! There's a list of sites in the "Internet Resources" section below, but you can just search for chess sites yourself and come up with hundreds in an instant.

MORE CHESS PROBLEMS

You can find answers on page 113.

PROBLEM 1

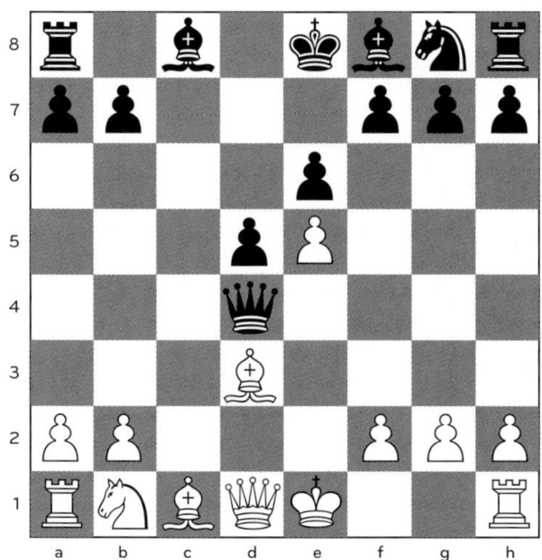

How can White use a discovered attack to win material?

PROBLEM 2

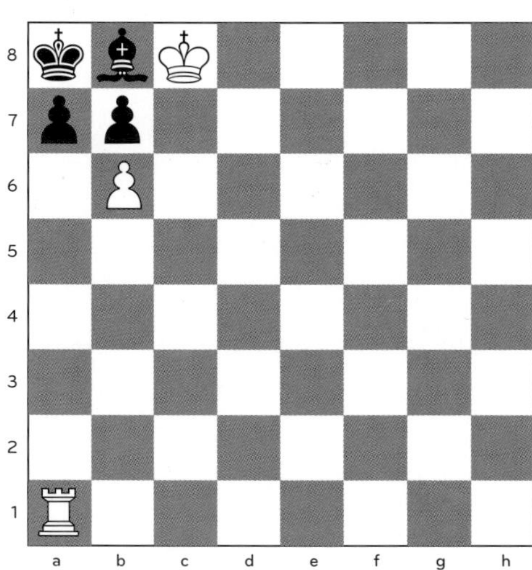

An unexpected move here will allow White to checkmate in his following move. What is the move?

PROBLEM 3

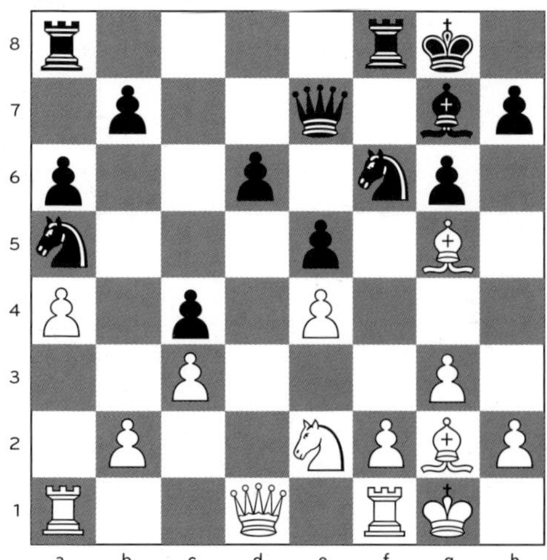

How can White use a double attack to win material? (Hint: It takes two moves.)

PROBLEM 4

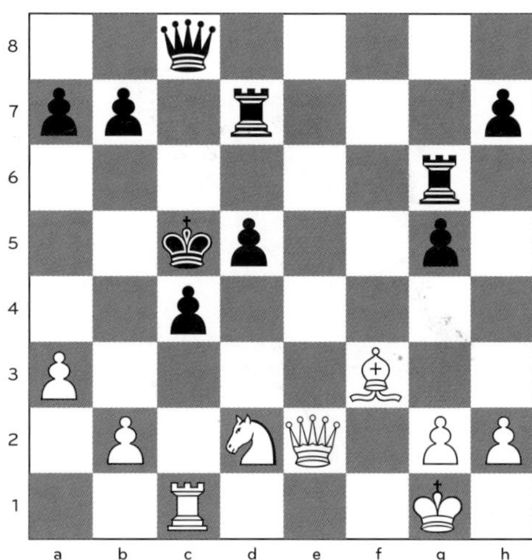

How can White use a skewer to win material?

CONCLUSION

We hope this book has gotten you interested in becoming a chess player, at least for fun if not for serious competition. If you're lucky, some of your friends and family already play the game, and you'll have plenty of local competition to sharpen your skills against. If not, remember that it's a wide world and the Internet, chess clubs, computer programs, books, and newspapers are all available at your fingertips.

So, General, as we bid you good-bye, we wish you good luck in battle. You'll surely win some and lose some, but either way, we hope you'll enjoy playing "the Royal Game," as millions of others have over the centuries. Video games may come and go, but remember—there'll always be chess!

GLOSSARY

Use these terms to help you navigate the book, as well as the chess board!

Attack a move, or series of moves, that puts the opponent's pawns, pieces, or position in jeopardy. The opponent must try and defend himself or counterattack if able to.

Back rank a player's home rank, where his pieces begin the game. A **back-rank mate** is where one player advances a queen or rook to the opponent's back rank, checking the king, which cannot escape because it is blockaded by its own pawns.

Backward pawn a lone undeveloped pawn, or a pawn at the rear of a pawn chain, with no other pawn to protect it.

BCA/BCF British Chess Association/British Chess Federation.

Blindfold chess chess played without one or both players being able to see the board. Actual blindfolds were once involved, but nowadays the players mostly just sit with their backs to the board. They follow the game by both players saying aloud the notation for their moves.

Blitz chess *(speed chess, lightning chess)* a chess game where the players have a very short time, normally 5 minutes, to complete all their moves in the game.

Capture the taking of one pawn or piece by an opposing piece or pawn, by moving onto its square (except in the case of "en passant")

Castling a special move where the king and rook bypass one another to reach their new squares. This is great for defending your king.

Center the squares d4, d5, e4, and e5.

Check an attack on the king by a piece or pawn. The king must move, or the attacking piece must be blocked or captured.

Checkmate a check that cannot be escaped. Checkmate ends the game.

Chess clock a clock with two separate faces that keeps time for both players in a tournament game.

Chess problem a diagrammed chess position that challenges you to find the right move to win the game for one side or the other.

Closed file a file with at least one pawn of each color on it.

Closed game or position one that begins with White's **1. d4**. These games tend to result in middle games where maneuvering is difficult because pawns are interlocked, blocking both sides from advancing, and there is limited room for all-out attacks.

Combination a forced sequence of moves that results in victory or great advantage for the player who executes it.

Correspondence chess a chess game played by two players at a great distance via mail or e-mail.

Decoy sacrifice a move that forces an opponent's piece into a square where it will be captured.

Deflection a move that forces a piece away from the defense of an important square.

Development the advancement of pieces from their starting squares.

Diagonal a line of squares along which the bishop and queen can move. In notation, it is identified by the squares at either end of the diagonal (e.g. a1–h8).

Diagram a drawing of a chess position.

Discovered attack an attack on an opposing piece that occurs when a pawn or piece is moved out of the way.

Discovered check an attack on the king that occurs when a pawn or piece is moved out of the way.

Double check/attack when two pieces or pawns attack the opponent's king/piece at the same time.

Doubled pawns two pawns of the same color that occupy the same file.

Draw a game that ends with neither side winning. Can occur a number of different ways.

Endgame the latter part of a chess game, when most of the pieces and pawns have already been captured. Not every chess game makes it this far.

En passant a special move where one pawn captures another after its first move (of two squares only), by moving diagonally forward to the square directly behind the captured pawn.

En prise a pawn or piece that can be captured without paying a material price.

Escape square *(flight square, luft)* a place for the king to go if it is attacked on the back rank.

Exchange To exchange (verb) means to trade pawns or pieces, not necessarily of equal value. The exchange (noun) refers to the loss of a knight or bishop in exchange for an opposing rook.

Fianchetto a maneuver that allows a bishop to be developed on the squares b2, b7, g2, or g7, and attack the center from the flank.

FIDE Federacion Internationale des Echecs—the International Chess Federation.

File any of the eight rows on the chessboard going vertically from White side to Black side and back. In notation, marked by the letters **a–h**.

Flanks the sides of the board.

Fool's Mate the quickest mate in chess.

Fork situation where two pieces of one color are attacked by one of the opposite color at the same time.

Gambit a planned sacrifice in the opening.

Grandmaster the top rank of players, awarded by FIDE.

Initiative the advantage you get when you are in control of the action, forcing your opponent to respond to your moves rather than making plans of his own.

International master FIDE designation for the rank below grandmaster.

Isolated pawn a pawn with no pawns of its own color on adjacent files to support it—a weak position.

Kibitzer someone who watches a game and comments as it goes on, in the range of hearing of the players. An amateur. Not a serious player.

Kingside the **e**, **f**, **g**, and **h** files.

Living chess a game on a very large board where real people act as the pawns and pieces.

Luft an escape square for a castled king.

Major piece a queen or rook.

Master ranking below international master.

Match a contest between two players playing multiple games.

Mate checkmate, for short.

Material pawns and pieces.

Middle game after the opening and before the endgame. The pieces are developed, and the battle is on!

Minor piece a knight or bishop.

Mobility the ability to move your pieces around the board quickly and easily to wherever you need them.

Notation the system of writing down and reading chess moves.

Open file a file that has no pawns on it.

Open game one that begins with **1. e4...e5**. This tends to produce a middle-game where the position is fluid and both players have good mobility to plan and carry out attacks.

Opening the first part of a chess game, when the players advance their pawns and develop their pieces.

Passed pawn one with no enemy pawn on its file or the files next to it. Good to have, especially in the endgame.

Pawn one of sixteen foot soldiers, eight to a side, that begin the game on the second rank from the rear on either side. They move only forward, capture only diagonally, and can be converted to any piece upon reaching the farthest rank.

Pawn chain a row of pawns, along one or more diagonals, that protect one another.

Pawn promotion when a pawn reaches the back rank, and can be exchanged for any piece, usually the queen.

Perpetual check when one player can keep the other in check indefinitely without a checkmate. This results in a draw by the rule of three-time repetition of a position.

Piece a queen, rook, bishop, knight, or king.

Pin when a piece or pawn is under attack and, if it moves, a major piece is threatened.

Queenside the **a**, **b**, **c**, and **d** files.

Rank any of the eight rows on the chessboard going horizontally left to right, or vice versa. In notation, marked by the numbers **1–8**.

Rating a score that shows how far advanced a chess player you are. In tournaments, you are "seeded," or ranked, according to your rating.

Resigning when one player tips his or her king over, gets up, shakes hands, and concedes the game.

Sacrifice a deliberate loss of material in order to gain something else (initiative, attacking possibilities, positional advantage, open files or diagonals, or material gain down the line).

Scholar's Mate a four-move chess game where a queen and bishop capture the opposing pawn on the f file, resulting in checkmate.

Semi-open game one where White starts off with **1. e4**, but Black responds with something other than **1. ...e5**. These games tend to result in unbalanced, or "asymmetrical" positions. Typical of a semi-open game is the Sicilian Defense (see p.53).

Simultaneous chess when a player plays more than one game, and usually several games, at once.

Skewer an attack on an opponent's piece where, if that piece moves, a minor piece or pawn can be captured. The opposite of a *pin.*

Stalemate when one player has no legal move, but is not in checkmate. This results in a draw.

Staunton chessmen the standard chess set of modern times.

Strategy long-term planning. Thinking far ahead.

Tactics a short series of moves that results in an advantage to the player.

Tempo the Latin word for "time." If you lose one tempo, you surrender the initiative. The more you lose them, the worse off you are.

Touch move the rule in chess: if you touch a pawn or piece, you MUST move it if legally possible.

Tournament a chess competition with more than two competitors, it can take different forms. A round robin is where every player plays every other player once, and the player with the best record wins. The Swiss System pairs players based on ratings in successive rounds until there is a winner. A match, by contrast, is a competition between two players.

Trade a mutual capturing of pieces of equal value.

USCF the U.S. Chess Federation, governing body of U.S. chess.

Winning the exchange giving up a knight or bishop and getting a rook.

Zugzwang a position in which there is no good move to make.

BIBLIOGRAPHY

Alburt, Lev. *Chess Training Pocket Book.* Chess Information Research Center, 2000.

Alburt, Lev and Krogius, Nikolai. *Just the Facts!* Chess Information Research Center, 2000.

Berg, Barry, *Opening Moves: The Making of a Young Chess Champion.* Little, Brown & Co., 2000.

Burgess, Graham. *The Mammoth Book of Chess.* Robinson, 1997.

Chandler, Murray. *How to Beat Your Dad at Chess.* Gambit, 2006 edition.

Chernev, Irving. *Logical Chess, Move by Move.* Simon and Schuster, 1957.

De Firmian, Nick. *Modern Chess Openings.* McKay, 1999.

Eade, James. *Chess for Dummies, 2nd edition.* Wiley, 2005.

———. *Chess Player's Bible.* Barron's, 2004.

Fischer, Bobby, Marguiles, Stuart, and Mosenfelder, Donn. *Bobby Fischer Teaches Chess.* Bantam, 1966.

Hooper and Whyld. *The Oxford Companion to Chess, 2nd edition.* Oxford University Press, 1992.

Howard, Kenneth S. *The Enjoyment of Chess Problems.* Dover, 1961.

King, Daniel. *Chess, From First Moves to Checkmate.* Kingfisher, 2000.

Kmoch, Hans, annotator. *Rubinstein's Chess Masterpieces—100 selected games.* Dover, 1941.

Lasker, Edward. *Chess Strategy.* Dover, 1959.

Lasker, Emmanuel. *How to Play Chess.* Bell, 1925.

Pachman, Ludek and Russell. A.S. *Modern Chess Strategy.* Gambit, 1998.

Pandolfini, Bruce. *Treasure Chess.* Random House, 2007.

Reinfeld, Fred. *Fifth Book of Chess: How to Win When You're Ahead.* Sterling, 1955.

Reti, Richard. *Modern Ideas in Chess.* Dover, 1960.

PHOTO CREDITS

Alekhine at Margate Chess Congress @ Hulton-Deutsch Collection/CORBIS, 88
Chess Game Between Bobby Fischer and Boris Spassky @ Bettmann/CORBIS, 88
Chess Player Mikhail Botvinnik @ Hulton-Deutsch Collection/CORBIS, 88
Men Playing a Game of Chess @ Bettmann/CORBIS, 88
World Chess Championship @ Mernandez Bianchi/Sygma/CORBIS, 88
Karpov Plays Chess @ Vittoriano Rastelli/CORBIS, 95
Capablanca and Steiner in Novel Living Chess Game @ Hulton-Deutsch Collection/CORBIS, 98

INTERNET RESOURCES

Znosko-Borovsky, Eugene A. *How NOT to Play Chess.* Dover, 1949.

International Chess Federation
www.fide.com

U.S. Chess Federation
www.uschess.org

Chess Federation of Canada
www.chess.ca

The Chess Café
www.chesscafe.com

Your Move Chess & Games
www.chessusa.com

Play Chess Online (Fee)
www.playchess.com
www.chessclub.com

MSN's Chess Site
www.zone.com

Free Internet Chess
www.pogo.com
www.freechess.org

Yahoo Live Chess Games
http://Games.yahoo.com

Fee-based Online Chess
www.chesslive.org

The Week in Chess
www.chesscenter.com/twic/twic.html

Information on Computer Chess
en.wikipedia.org/wiki/Computer_chess

Electronic chess instruction
www.chess.com
www.chessbase.com
www.chesscafe.com
www.chessusa.com

Chess Databases
www.chessbase.com
www.chesscafe.com
www.chessusa.com
www.chessgames.com

General Information
http://chess.about.com
www.pitt.edu/-schach
www.chesscenter.com/twic/twic.html

ANSWERS TO CHESS PROBLEMS

Page 27—Check, Checkmate, or Stalemate

1. Black to move is in stalemate.
2. Black cannot move to a safe square and therefore is in checkmate.
3. Black is only in check since he can capture the queen with his king.
4. Black to move is still stalemate because while Black has a pawn in addition to a king, neither piece can move.

Page 59—Chess Problems from the Opening

Problem 1

While **3. Nf3** is a perfectly good move, **3. e4** gaining complete control of the central squares and threatening **Bxc4** is the cleanest approach.

Problem 2

As seen on page 53, **5. Nxe5** would not win a pawn for free since Black could play **5. ...Qd4**. Here, however, White is castled. Therefore he now threatens **6. Nxe5**. Black must either defend it directly with a move like **5. ...f6**, or indirectly with a move such as **5. ...Bg4**, creating a pin which effectively prevents **Nxe5**.

Problem 3

It is best to move the White knight to b5 where is gets control of the d6 square immediately.

Problem 4

White is controlling the center and prepares **4. e4**. Black can play **3. ...d5** which then becomes the Queen's Gambit Declined, which is discussed on page 55.

Page 79—Chess Problems from the Middle Game

Problem 1

White could trade off his potential weakness (the isolated queen pawn) by playing **d5** or playing for an attack on the king-side with moves like **Ba2**, then **Bb1**. As a rule, the side with the isolated pawn should trade off the major pieces (queens and rooks). The side without the isolated pawn should trade the minor pieces (bishops and knights).

Problem 2

Black should attack on the king-side with **...Ne8**, then **...f5**, and then **...f4**. White should advance on the Queen-side with **b4** and then **c5**. As a general rule, one wants to push the pawn next to one's furthest advanced pawn.

Problem 3

White should start with **h3** (preventing **Bg4**). Black, in turn, should plan to challenge White's coming central domination. He can do that with **...Na5** followed by **...c5**.

Problem 4

A good move for White here is **Bf4**. In addition to preventing Black from playing the move **...e5**, White also threatens to trade off his dark-squared bishop for Black's better dark-squared bishop. Good and bad bishops are usually determined by what color squares one's own central pawns occupy. In the above positions, Black has his central pawns on light squares. These block his light-squared bishop from moving freely, which is why that bishop is considered "bad."

Page 99

Problem 1: Admired by Lenin

1. Kb7!! If Black promotes his pawn and makes a queen, White moves

2. Bf8 Checkmate! If Black sees the mate and simply moves his king away, White's bishop captures Black's pawn, and covers a1 so Black can no longer earn a pawn promotion. From here on in, White's advantages are too strong for Black to overcome.

Problem 2: Smyth vs. Helms

1. ...Qg2+! Helms's queen sacrifice produces an incredible checkmate:

2. Kxg2...Rxg3#!!

Page 103—More Chess Problems

Problem 1

Bb5 check wins the Black queen.

Problem 2

1. Ra6. Then, if **...bxa6**, then **2. b7#**. On any bishop move, **Rxa7** is a checkmate.

Problem 3

Bxf6. Even after a counter-capture of White's bishop on f6, White's next move, **Qd5#**, is a double attack on the Black king on g8 and Black knight on a5.

Problem 4

Rxc4...dxc4 then **Qxc4** skewers the Black king to the White queen and also wins Black's queen.

INDEX